Studies in Economics and Business Administration

Published under the Direction of the
GRADUATE SCHOOL OF BUSINESS
ADMINISTRATION
THE UNIVERSITY OF NORTH CAROLINA
AT CHAPEL HILL

Volume 6

Studies in Economics and Business Administration

previously published

Pareto's Methodological Approach to Economics

A Study in the History of Some Scientific Aspects of Economic Thought

Pareto's Methodological Approach to Economics

A STUDY IN THE HISTORY OF SOME SCIENTIFIC
ASPECTS OF ECONOMIC THOUGHT

by
Vincent J. Tarascio

THE UNIVERSITY OF NORTH CAROLINA PRESS
CHAPEL HILL

Copyright © 1966, 1968 by
The University of North Carolina Press
Manufactured in the United States of America
Library of Congress Catalog Card Number 67-65595
Printed by the William Byrd Press, Inc.

To my wife, Linda

Acknowledgments

This work is the consequence of a doctoral dissertation in economics written at Rice University. I owe a debt of gratitude to the members of my thesis committee, Professors Gaston V. Rimlinger, Marian Krzyzaniak, and Louis H. Mackey, for their helpful criticisms and suggestions. I am also indebted to Professor Hans Jaksch, who first excited my interest in Pareto's doctrines, and to Professor Jacques Melitz for his introduction to methodology.

Finally, there is my wife, Linda, whose encouragement, as well as patience and assistance with several drafts of this manuscript, was greatly responsible for its successful completion.

Chapel Hill, North Carolina
April, 1967

Table of Contents

Pareto's Methodological Approach to Economics

A Study in the History of Some Scientific Aspects of Economic Thought

I *Introduction*

The more common approach to the study of economic thought has been through examination of the economic doctrines written and taught by economists, or through the study of certain analytical aspects of these doctrines. Schumpeter's monumental work, *History of Economic Analysis,* is essentially a study in the history of the analytical aspects of economic science.[1] One need only contrast this work with that of Gide and Rist, *A History of Economic Doctrines,* to appreciate the differences of approach and emphasis in the study of the history of economic thought.[2] On the other hand, discussions of scope and method have been carried on rather independently of doctrine, the concern often being an attempt to resolve differences as to the "proper" scientific method in economics.[3] In any case, the methodological interpretation of the procedures used by an author has received very little attention in the history of economic thought. The assumption seems to be that, given a mastery of the theoretical tools of economics, the economic doctrines of an author are plain for everyone to see. Unfortunately this belief is erroneous, for a failure to understand an author's views on scope and method often results in a failure to understand the economic doctrines themselves.[4] This is so

1. Joseph Schumpeter, *History of Economic Analysis* (New York: Oxford University Press, 1954). Of course, Schumpeter's work does not ignore doctrinal or methodological aspects. However, his main interest is in the development of economic analysis.

2. Charles Gide and Charles Rist, *A History of Economic Doctrines,* trans. R. Richards (2nd ed.; Boston: D. C. Heath & Co., 1948).

3. Unfortunately, the fact that discussions on scope and method have been carried on independently of economic doctrine has often resulted in the attitude among economists that such discussions have little to offer and are a waste of time.

4. For example, I shall show that Pareto's distinction between "ophelimity" and "utility" has been overlooked by historians of economic thought because

because an author's methodology influences his doctrine. Also, in order to understand fully an author's writings, one must be familiar with many aspects—biographical, theoretical, doctrinal, methodological, etc. It seems, therefore, that purely theoretical or doctrinal studies are not all that can be done in the field of economic thought, and that a study of methodological aspects should at least add to our knowledge by furnishing us with new insights into—and hence understanding of—an author's works.

An emphasis on methodological aspects should not be interpreted as a deprecation of the researches of those who have chosen a different course. In fact, all approaches, whether they be biographical, theoretical, doctrinal, methodological, etc., are not in opposition but are supplementary to each other. I have concentrated my attention on the methodological aspects of Pareto's economics and sociology with the attitude that therein lies not a universal method for the history of thought but merely an alternative approach to the understanding of Pareto's works. The fact that such studies have been so lacking in the history of thought is justification in itself for this approach.

During the nineteenth-century development of economics, there was a kind of intellectual interregnum during which the procedures used by economists were vague, shifting, and tentative. As economics developed, economists, as well as sociologists, felt the need to "rationalize" their aims and procedures. By the late nineteenth century, the issue of what economics was and whether it was a science had become significant, especially on the European continent.

The many currents and cross-currents of intellectual thought during the period make simple generalizations difficult. Nevertheless, it appears to me that several major methodological issues were involved in the differing views of the various intellectual traditions. These issues were ethical neutrality in the social sciences, the scope of economics and sociology, the nature and use of "generalizing" concepts in the social sciences, and the interplay of theory and empirical work.

The purpose of this study is to establish the place of Pareto in the contemporary methodological issues of his time, and to evaluate his contribution toward making economics more scientific. I shall show that his contribution was important not only in terms of improving

---

of their failure to understand his methodology. Also, I shall show that the supporters and critics of his so-called "refutation" of the marginal productivity theory seem to have imputed more to Pareto than he had in mind, for the same reason. However, the technical aspects of Pareto's economics and sociology are only of secondary importance in this study since such discussions serve merely as illustrations of his methodology.

the discipline, but also with regard to its acceptability as a guide to the policy maker. My choice of Pareto stems from the influence of his works on modern economic theory and the relevance of his methodological views even today.

Pareto's views on scope and method can best be presented in the context of the polemic, in which he was a participant, that took place during his time between the German historical economists and the advocates of economic theory. My approach is essentially historical although, of course, his views will be related to current problems whenever they are applicable.[5] During the course of research I found that many of Pareto's views on scope and method were similar to those of Max Weber, who represented a different intellectual tradition. The two authors' views will be compared. Certain of Pareto's views will also be contrasted with those of Alfred Marshall, the leading English economist of the period, who represented a different intellectual tradition from that of either Pareto or Weber.

This study will be organized according to the contemporary issues mentioned above. Chapter II will serve as an introduction to Pareto and his time. Chapter III will encompass the issue of ethical neutrality. Chapter IV will deal with the problem of the scope of economics and sociology. Chapter V will be primarily concerned with the general methodology of the social sciences. In particular, I shall focus attention on the nature and use of "generalizing" concepts in the social sciences. Chapter VI will deal with more specific economic topics concerning the interplay of economic theory and empirical work. Finally, in the concluding chapter a general assessment will be made of Pareto's methodology.

5. The question of a criterion by which to judge the relevance of some of the contemporary methodological issues of the nineteenth century is an important consideration in a study of this kind. From the modern perspective it may appear that some of the issues mentioned above have been resolved, and this is true to a certain extent. But the history of economics shows that it has been a much less cumulatively progressive science than meets the eye. For instance, the J. Stuart-Malthus-Marx-J. A. Hobson underconsumption doctrine was considered a dead issue by the contemporaries of these writers, as well as by later writers, only to be "rediscovered" by J. M. Keynes. Since doctrines also reflect the methodological orientation of writers, the current acceptance of the underconsumption doctrine implies the acceptance, to some extent, of methodological views that were once considered "erroneous." On the other hand, a purely "relativistic" interpretation—that ideas should be weighed sympathetically in the context of their times—may amount to little more than an apology for our predecessors or even ancestor worship. The latter approach hardly presents an environment for critical analysis. What is needed, then, is a compromise between the two approaches. In this study I shall take a position somewhere between the two extremes, although I must confess a "relativistic" tendency.

II *Pareto and His Time*

PARETO THE MAN: A BIOGRAPHICAL SKETCH

The Marquis Vilfredo Pareto was born in Paris, July 15, 1848, the son of Raffaele and Marie Mettenier Pareto.[1] The father, Raffaele, was living in France in voluntary exile, having been a partisan of the Mazzini movement. He had arrived in Paris at the age of twenty-four. Not having emigrated from Italy with any personal fortune, he competed for a position as a civil engineer. The report of the examiners qualified him as a "sujet des plus distingués par son instruction et d'une capacité remarquable."[2] He was called back to Italy in 1858 because of his proficiency in hydraulics, and the Pareto family settled in Turin, where Raffaele obtained a supervisory position on the Italian railways.

When of age, Vilfredo entered the Polytechnic Institute of Turin. While there he acquired a command of mathematics on a professional level. In 1869 he was graduated with a doctor's degree in engineering, having achieved first position in the final examination.[3] The title of his dissertation was—and this is mentioned because later he incorporated the same mathematical concepts into his general equilibrium analysis—"The Fundamental Principles of the Theory of Elasticity in Solid Bodies, and the Researches Concerning the Integration of the

1. There are many biographies of Pareto. The most worthwhile are: Luigi Amoroso, "Vilfredo Pareto," *Econometrica*, VI (Jan., 1938), 1-21; G. H. Bosquet, *Vilfredo Pareto, sa vie et son oeuvre* (Paris: Payot et Cie., 1928); Maffeo Pantaleoni, "Vilfredo Pareto," *Economic Journal*, XXXIII (Sept., 1923), 582-90; the "Biographical Note" by Arthur Livingston in Pareto, *The Mind and Society*, trans. and ed. A. Livingston (4 vols.; New York: Harcourt, Brace and Co., 1935), pp. xv-xviii; and Joseph Schumpeter, "Vilfredo Pareto (1848-1923)," *Quarterly Journal of Economics*, LXIII (May, 1949), 147-73.
2. Pantaleoni, *Economic Journal*, XXXIII, 589.
3. *Ibid.*, p. 584.

6

Differential Equations Determining their Equilibrium."[4] Upon receiving his degree, Pareto had to go to work for financial reasons. Hence he was unable to follow the career of a researcher in the physical sciences, in spite of his high standing in that field. His early training and experiences are important for their influence on his conceptual thinking, especially in mathematical economics and statistics, as well as on his views on scope and method.

The second, and most important, period in Pareto's intellectual development was the time during which he resided in Italy as a businessman. He began his business career in his father's footsteps, as a consulting engineer for the railways. He was employed at Rome for four years, and in 1874 was offered a position as general superintendent of the ironworks in Val d'Arno controlled by the Banca Nazional of Florence. He held that position for six years.[5]

Since his attention was drawn to such problems as production, labor, transportation, and customs duties, as well as to monetary and political problems, Pareto's experiences as a businessman were important in the development of his economic and political interests. Pantaleoni tells us that Pareto had "many scores of times" visited Great Britain, especially Scotland.[6] Pareto must have been immensely impressed with Britain's industrialization and economic growth; he sided with the friends of liberalism and free trade. He joined the Adam Smith Society founded by Ferrara in Florence and was an active member with DeJohannis, Martello, and others.[7] Pareto's early *laissez faire* sentiments were to be reflected in his early works, namely the *Cours d'économie politique*.[8] His first exposure to abstract economics seems to have been Pantaleoni's *Elementi di economia pura*.[9] In fact, it was Pantaleoni who first opened Pareto's eyes to the merits of Walras' work, of which Pareto had had a low opinion.[10] He later developed a deep and lasting friendship with the author of the *Elementi,* as evidenced by a three-volume collection of letters written to Pantaleoni, published in recent years.[11]

4. Published in: Vilfredo Pareto, *Scritti teorici*, Racotti da Giovanni Demaria (Milano: Rodolfo Malfasi Editone, 1953).

5. Pareto, *Mind and Society*, p. xvi.

6. Pantaleoni, *Economic Journal*, xxxiii, 588.

7. *Ibid.*

8. Vilfredo Pareto, *Cours d'économie politique* (2 vols.; Lausanne: Librairie de l'Université, 1897).

9. Amoroso, *Econometrica, VI,* 1. The *Elementi di economia pura* was first translated into English in 1898 and has recently been republished as: M. Pantaleoni, *Pure Economics* (New York: Kelly and Millman, 1957).

10. Pareto, *Mind and Society*, p. xviii.

11. Vilfredo Pareto, *Lettere a Maffeo Pantaleoni 1890-1923,* A cura di Gabriele De Rosa (3 vols.; Roma: Edizioni di Storia e Litteratura, 1962).

Pareto's interest in other scientific and intellectual fields continued to develop. While in Florence he acquired his knowledge of Greek and history and became a learned classical scholar. He translated the Greek Anthology for pleasure, and even attempted a comparative analysis of the language of Saint Paul and the Attic dialect.[12] In addition to Italian, he knew French, English, Latin, and Greek.[13] Pareto made decisive friendships with such persons as Domenico Comparetti, the famous philologist and Hellenist; Arturo Linacher, a learned classicist; Sydney Sonnino, the statesman; and Giustino Fortunato, the biographer. He was also a friend of A. Franchetti, who was then working on a translation of Aristophanes. They were all members of a group which gathered at the house of Peruzzi, the meeting place of some of the most brilliant minds of that period in Florence. This was the period during which Pareto came under the influence of Auguste Comte's philosophy of positivism and his writings on sociology. Like Comte, Pareto later come to despise metaphysics and transcendentalism, and many of his later views on scientific methodology had their origins in the "Italian period" of his life.

Pareto became deeply involved in politics during his days in Italy. He attacked the protectionist policy of the time, and even stood for Parliament for the district of Pistoria on a free-trade platform.[14] He was defeated. He was appalled by what seemed to him political incompetence and corruption in Italy, and he fought the governments that succeeded each other until he became known as an ultraliberal— an uncompromising advocate of *laissez faire*.[15] However, his was a peculiar kind of *laissez faire*, entirely at variance with that of the English. In his attacks upon protectionism and parliamentary democracy, Pareto was running counter to the popular political sentiments of the times, a practice which resulted in his political and social isolation. Schumpeter maintains that Pareto's "patrician" background prevented him from establishing emotional relations with the parliamentary democratic creations of the bourgeois mind.[16]

12. Amoroso, *Econometrica, VI,* 2.
13. There is some dispute as to Pareto's knowledge of German. He was familiar with the German literature in economics and gives many references to the original German editions in his writings. G. Eisermann, *Vilfredo Pareto als Nationalökonom und Soziologe* (Tübingen: Mohr, 1961), pp. 56-57, assumes that Pareto knew German. On the other hand, Norberto Bobbio, "Introduction to Pareto's Sociology," *Banca Nazional del Lavoro, Quarterly Review,* No. 69 (June, 1964), p. 192, disagrees with Eisermann, adding that "Pareto despised everything German."
14. Pareto, *Mind and Society,* p. xvi.
15. Schumpeter, *Quarterly Journal of Economics,* LXIII, 152.
16. *Ibid.,* p. 151.

Regardless of the reasons, it seemed that Pareto preferred to live apart from the mainstream of Italian politics. Upon the death of his father in 1882, he was able to retire, together with his wife and mother, to Villa Rosa in Fusole. He was then thirty-four years of age. He intended to prepare himself for a professorship in economics. For eleven long years he was unable to secure the position he sought in Italy, although his articles in the *Academia dei Georgofili,* the *Economista di Firenza,* the *Journal des Economistes,* and the *Giornale degli economisti* attracted wide attention. Finally, he accepted an offer in 1893 to succeed Walras in the chair of Political Economy at the University of Lausanne.

Pareto's experiences in Italy had a great influence upon him. His training in mathematics and the physical sciences, his experience in business, and his great interest in current issues of economic and general policy are all-important in understanding the man and his works.

To the disappointment of Walras, his successor at Lausanne was one whose philosophy and practical recommendations were at complete odds with his own. According to Schumpeter, although their pure theories were cast in the same mold, their systems of thought and their visions of the social process differed.[17] Walras' philosophy was that of "petty-bourgeois radicalism," derived from the "semi-socialist" French writers together with equal justice from utilitarianism.[18] Pareto had had enough of reform schemes in Italy, so he was determined to establish economics on "scientific" grounds devoid, as far as possible, of ethical considerations. As time passed a deep-seated mutual dislike developed between the two personalities, which even spread to third parties.[19]

Pareto's own earlier "unscientific" proclivities became a source of personal embarrassment to him, and his intellectual honesty caused him to be as critical of his own earlier works as he was of those of others. He paid no court to "isms" and maintained an ethical neutrality, attacking his personal supporters as well as his critics when he felt that they were expounding some favored system of ethics. To those who find comfort in pinning one mantle or another on a writer,

17. *Ibid.,* p. 155.
18. The ethical aspects of Walras' doctrines will be discussed in the following chapter.
19. For a discussion of the personalities see: T. Giacalone-Monaco, *Pareto-Walras da un carteggio inedito (1891-1901)* (Padova: Cedam, 1957). Pareto's experiences with the administration at Lausanne are given by G. Busino, "Pareto e le autorità di Losanna," *Giornale degli economisti,* N.S. XXII (March-April, 1963), 260-303.

Pareto seems inconsistent—the former advocate of *laissez faire* now attacking and even ridiculing the "ethical systems" of his old comrades.[20] They fail to realize that the criterion by which Pareto was judging such systems of thought was, as we shall see later, the "scientific" basis of these systems. Pareto was just as critical of the adulators of Marx, and for this reason he was incorrectly named the "bourgeois" Karl Marx. Considering his attacks on both the "right" and the "left," it seems rather amazing that he was able to accomplish what Walras had not: he founded a school, the Lausanne school, supported by such eminent scholars as Pantaleoni, Barone, Amoroso, and Borgatta.[21] As is the case with such schools of thought, Pareto had the misfortune of creating *Epigoni,* who did more harm than good, who strained his theories, by blindly defending what they rarely understood and using him as a springboard for themselves. As Pantaleoni observed, every great man has had to labor under the inconvenience of such persons, whose "schools" more properly are "obnoxious syndicates of fools."[22]

In 1906 Pareto resigned his chair at Lausanne and retired to his country home on Lake Geneva, where he became known as the "lone thinker of Celigny." It was here at "Villa Angora" that Pareto published, in Italian, his great work in economics, *Manuale d'economia politica* (1906),[23] and his famous work in sociology, *Trattato di sociologia generale* (1916).[24] This was his most fruitful period of study and meditation, commencing relatively late in life, when he was fifty-eight years of age.

Born of a French mother, he loved France. He was grateful to Switzerland, which gave him hospitality; but he was always, and above all, Italian. He loved Italy and remained an Italian national even in his adopted land. As soon as he retired he reverted to writing in Italian, having written the *Cours* and *Les systèmes socialistes*[25] in

20. Werner Stark, "In Search of the True Pareto," *British Journal of Sociology,* XIV (June, 1963), 103-12, is one such writer who accuses Pareto of being inconsistent.
21. Pantaleoni, *Economic Journal,* xxxiii, 589.
22. *Ibid.,* p. 590.
23. Vilfredo Pareto, *Manuale d'economia politica* (Milano: Società editrice libraria, 1906). French translation and revision: *Manuel d'économie politique* (Paris: Giard et Brière, 1909). Because the mathematical appendix in the *Manuale* was completely revised in the French edition, it will be necessary to cite the French edition on occasion.
24. Vilfredo Pareto, *Trattato di sociologia generale* (4 vols.; Barbera, 1916). The *Trattato* was translated into English as *The Mind and Society,* cited above.
25. Vilfredo Pareto, *Les systèmes socialistes* (2 vols.; Paris: Giard et Brière, 1902-3).

French, the language of Lausanne, out of courtesy to the university.

During his earlier life the governments of Italy had paid no attention to him. Now he had reached an eminence in his beloved country which bordered on reverence. The Fascist Government made him a Senator of the Kingdom, together with his great friend Pantaleoni. He was nominated as Italy's delegate to the League of Nations, but his health precluded acceptance.

Pareto was an independent, but the honors bestowed upon him by a fascist state, together with the attempt of Mussolini to find an intellectual basis for his doctrines in Pareto's works, have led to some speculation as to Pareto's being the precursor of fascism. Yet Bosquet points out that in one of the last of his newspaper articles he warned the new fascist government *against* warlike adventures, restriction of the freedom of the press and opinion, punitive taxation of the rich and peasants, alliances with the Church, and any infringement of freedom of teaching in the universities.[26] History has shown that the fascist regime ignored Pareto completely. As early as 1924, Alberto Cappa strove to show in a monograph not merely Pareto's neutrality in the face of the vicissitudes of his time, but also the impossibility of finding any confirmation that he favored authoritarianism.[27] More recently, the editor of a combative antifascist review of the 1920's, Oliviero Zuccarini, has written an *apologia pro* Pareto, defending Pareto against all posthumous accusations and generously presenting him as a faithful friend of democracy.[28]

PARETO: THE ECONOMIST AND THE SOCIOLOGIST

Pareto's period of active economic research was 1892-1912, after which he devoted his complete interest to sociology. He lived in a period in which both economics and sociology were in a state of ferment. In economics, the French and English liberal schools, defending the doctrine of classical political economy, had been attacked on the one hand by the German historical economists and on the other hand by the followers of Marx.[29]

26. Cf. Bosquet, *Vilfredo Pareto,* p. 193.
27. A Cappa, *Vilfredo Pareto* (Torino: Gobetti, 1924), pp. 12-13, 66-67. See Bobbio, *Banca Nazional del Lavoro, Quarterly Review,* No. 69, pp. 201-2, for a further discussion of the fascists' attempts to use Pareto's theories as a source of their doctrines.
28. O. Zuccarini, "Politica e sociologia di Vilfredo Pareto," *Comunità,* No. 94 (Nov. 15, 1961), pp. 84-101.
29. What is of interest for the purpose of this study is that, very often, the basis for controversy among antagonistic schools of thought was ethical. The ethical aspects of economic doctrine will be discussed in the following chapter.

The marginal utility theories of Jevons, Menger, and Walras gave rise to marginal analysis and the application of the "maximization principle" not only to demand theory but also to supply theory. With the exception of the Austrians—Menger, Wieser, and Böhm-Bawerk—who opposed the use of mathematics on methodological grounds,[30] the greatest of the so-called "literary" economic theorists of the period had at least some training in mathematics, i.e., Jevons, Marshall, Wicksteed, Wicksell, and Cassel. Of these, Marshall and Wicksell possessed a better technical mathematical competence. Other economists such as Cournot, Walras, Edgeworth, Fisher, and Pareto were avowedly mathematical economists. Economic theory during the period 1870-1914 developed along different lines in England and on the Continent. Marshall developed his *Principles*[31] with an emphasis on partial equilibrium analysis, while Walras developed his general equilibrium analysis in the *Eléments*.[32] Pareto followed in the tradition of Walras, and his "pure" economic theory is essentially the theory of general economic equilibrium.

Later, Pareto broke away from the marginal utility economists and proceeded to establish his own school—the Lausanne school. Many important developments in theoretical economics are now seen to stem from him. His contributions of particular note are: his "utility" and production theories, which form part of the foundation of modern demand and production analysis, together with their corresponding general equilibrium models; the new welfare economics (of which he is often referred to as the founder); and the income distribution curve (a pioneering effort in econometrics) more generally known today in econometric studies as the Pareto distribution.

However, Pareto owes a great deal to his predecessors and contemporaries, and those who seem to have influenced him the most are Cournot, Jevons, Walras, Edgeworth, and Fisher.[33] Moreover, the early influences of Ferrara and Pantaleoni were also important. It was mentioned earlier that Pareto was supported by such competent economists as Pantaleoni, Barone, Amoroso, and Borgatta, who

30. Menger, for example, objected to mathematics because it prevented the economists from getting to the qualitative "essence" of value, rent, and profit. Cf. M. Blaug, *Economic Theory in Retrospect* (Homewood, Ill.: Irwin, 1962), p. 275.

31. Alfred Marshall, *Principles of Economics* (1st ed. 1890; 8th ed.; London: Macmillan & Co., 1925).

32. Léon Walras, *Eléments d'économie politique pure* (1st ed. 1874; 4th [definitive] ed.; Paris: Pichon et Durand-Auzias, 1926). English translation: *Elements of Pure Economics,* trans. William Jaffé (Homewood, Ill.: Irwin, 1954).

33. Pantaleoni, *Economic Journal* XXXIII, 583.

helped to "popularize" his works. Later, Pareto's popularity among economists spread outside the Continent, largely through the efforts of Hicks and Allen in England and Schultz and Samuelson in the United States.[34] Yet in spite of his great popularity among theorists, and the present general textbook treatments of his theories in introductory and intermediate texts as well as in advanced texts in economics, his major works in economics have not been translated into English.

Turning now to sociology, we find the situation altogether different. For one thing, with the exception of what might be called a Pareto vogue in the United States, which occurred with the translation of the *Trattato* into English in the 1930's, the greatness of the structure as a whole has rarely been sensed outside of Europe. This is particularly puzzling since such competent sociologists as Parsons and Sorokin admired Pareto's sociology.[35] Sorokin felt, indeed, that the greatest contemporary sociologists had been Max Weber, Durkheim, and Pareto.[36] Even as early as 1923, Pantaleoni observed that Pareto's sociology was less known than his economics. Altogether the sociology had not been translated into English at the time, Pantaleoni felt this to be no obstacle to acquaintance since Pareto's economic works were never translated either. Perhaps an explanation is that Pareto was an economist turned sociologist. He attempted to use the same analytical concepts of economics, e. g., mutual dependence and equilibrium, in sociology. The "static-mechanistic" devices of economics were never popular with sociologists who were interested in dynamic-organic processes, and many of the later critiques of Pareto's sociology by sociologists have made this distinction.[37]

Moreover, Pareto's sociology is more correctly a sociology of the political process. This is quite understandable in view of Pareto's

34. J. R. Hicks, *Value and Captial* (Oxford: Clarendon Press, 1939); R. G. D. Allen, *Mathematical Analysis for Economists* (London: Macmillan & Co., 1938); Henry Schultz, "Marginal Productivity and the Pricing Process," *Journal of Political Economy,* XXXVII (Oct., 1929), 505-51; Paul A. Samuelson, *Foundations of Economic Analysis* (Cambridge, Mass.: Harvard, 1947). The influence of Pareto seems less direct in the *Foundations* than in the other works cited. However, there is more of Pareto in it than meets the eye, particularly in the sections on methodology, marginal productivity, and welfare economics. With respect to welfare economics, all modern welfare theory, including Samuelson's contribution, is homage to Pareto.
35. Talcott Parsons, *The Structure of Social Action* (York, Pa.: McGraw-Hill, 1937), pp. 178-300.
36. Bobbio, *Banca Nazional del Lavoro, Quarterly Review,* No. 69, p. 198.
37. More recent critics of the "static-mechanistic" character of Pareto's sociology have been Bobbio, *Banca Nazional del Lavoro, Quarterly Review,* No. 69, pp. 201-2, and Stark, *British Journal of Sociology,* XIV, 103-12.

early political experiences in Italy. According to Schumpeter, Pareto realized through his experiences that "everything man does or thinks or feels and all his cultural creations and his attitudes towards cultural creation are bound to come in somehow or other" in the political process, so that the latter becomes a special case of the former consideration.[38] This particular aspect of study might not be so important to the sociologist who approaches the study of social phenomena in a socio-cultural framework (although it is important in political sociology), but it was extremely important to Pareto, the economist, who was interested in the political implications of economic theory—economic policy. In this sense, although one must dig deeply to find evidence of it, Pareto's work was an "economic sociology." This fact can only be recognized when one studies *all* of Pareto's works and senses the development of Pareto's thoughts over time. However, his sociology is not "economic" because there is a great deal of economics in it; it is "economic" because it represents a logical development from pure economic theory, characteristic of Pareto's economics, to "policy," which Pareto felt was a "sociological" problem. What is surprising is that Pareto's sociology is hardly known among economists, especially in view of its relevance to the modern emphasis on all forms of policy: monetary, fiscal, development, etc. In these, the "economic" aspects of Pareto's sociology, there remains much to be discovered.[39]

38. Schumpeter, *Quarterly Journal of Economics*, LXIII, 168.
39. There is a very interesting analogy between Pareto's views on sociology (for economic policy) and the modern theory of the public household built around modern welfare theory, which in turn is built around Pareto's ophelimity theory. The modern theory of the public household is an offshoot of Pareto's views not only because of his welfare theory, but also because both Pareto and some modern writers (as well as Wicksell and Lindahl) ultimately turned to the analysis of the political process on matters of policy. For instance, budget determination through voting has received much attention in recent writings. Cf. Howard R. Bowen, *Toward Social Economy* (New York: Rinehart, 1948); K. Arrow, *Social Choice and Individual Values* (New York: John Wiley & Sons, 1951); Duncan Black, "On the Rationale of Group Decision-making," *Journal of Political Economy*, LVI (Feb., 1948), 23-24; "The Decision of a Committee Using a Special Majority," *Econometrica*, XVI (July, 1948), 245-61; "Wicksell's Principle in the Distribution of Taxation," *Economic Essays in Commemoration of the Dundee School of Economics*, ed. J. K. Eastman (London: Culross & Sons, 1955); Clifford Hildreth, "Alternative Condition of Social Ordering," *Econometrica*, XXI (Jan., 1953), 81-94; James M. Buchanan, "The Pure Theory of Government Finance: A Suggested Approach," *Journal of Political Economy*, LVII (Dec., 1949), 496-505; "Social Choice, Democracy and Free Markets," *Journal of Political Economy*, LXII (Apr., 1954), 114-23; R. A. Dahl and C. E. Lindblom, *Politics, Economics and Welfare* (New York: Harper & Brothers, 1953). What is important here is that although Pareto's method (and approach to policy) differs

In sociology, Pareto seems to have been influenced by the works of Machiavelli, Comte, Spencer, Darwin, and Bain. He also had a very high regard for Marx, especially for the Marxian concept of class conflict, and held Georges Sorel in very high esteem. Among others to whom Pareto felt that he owed a debt of gratitude were Ostragorski and Michels for their analysis of political parties; Lombroso and Ferri for criminal sociology; Colajanni, Fustel de Coulanges, and Henry Sumner Maine for "historical sociologies"; and Benedetto Croce, the philosopher.[40]

Pareto died on August 19, 1923, in Celigny. He had been married twice, the first time unhappily. He found domestic peace in his second wife—Jane Regis—to whom he dedicated the *Trattato.*

THE INTELLECTUAL BACKGROUND OF THE PERIOD 1850-1914

In this section my main concern will be with a survey of the intellectual character of the period in which Pareto lived. Very often, the methodological views of economists and sociologists reflect their intellectual orientations. This survey will serve toward bringing out the methodological conflict that surrounded social science and called its scientific status into question.

Before going on to discuss the main currents of intellectual thought, perhaps it will be best to begin with a statement regarding the methodological issues, which often remained implicit. These issues will be merely mentioned at this point, since they will be brought out in the main discussion.

First, the role of ethical judgments in the social sciences was a matter of great concern. The question as to whether the social sciences should or could be free of ethical considerations was highly debated.

---

from those of modern writers, their methodology is quite similar because policy is discussed within the broader political framework. This point will be discussed in greater detail in Chapter IV.

40. Cf. *Jubilé du professor V. Pareto* (Lausanne: Lausanne University, 1920), p. 56. Pantaleoni has observed that some suggestions of parts of Pareto's sociology are found in Gustave Le Bon's *Psychologie du socialisme* and *Psychologie de l'évolution des peuples,* Gaetano Mosca's *Principii di scienza politica,* and Paulhan's *Esprits logiques et ésprits faux* (Pantaleoni, *Economic Journal,* XXXIII, 589). Livingston, the translator of the *Trattato,* feels that Pareto owed a great deal to Comte for his methodology, to Bentham for his theory of "derivations," to Mosca for his theory of "class circulation," and to Frazer for his theory of "residues." These are merely mentioned here, and although researchers into the origins of a man's works are of intellectual interest, such considerations, in any great detail, are beyond the scope of this study.

Second, the scope of observation in social science researches was an important issue. Essentially, the controversy surrounding this issue centered on the atomistic versus the organistic conception of the social process. A third important issue focused attention on the role of factual observational data in the study of human society. In particular, there existed a great difference of opinion as to the role of empirical observation in the social sciences, the method of empirical observation (with or without a priori theory), and the trustworthiness of empirical observation (Marx). And finally, differing views regarding the meaning and verification of theory were reflected in the controversies during the period.[41]

A general survey of the intellectual character of the period in which Pareto lived presents several difficulties. For one thing, simple generalizations about thoughts of this time are extremely difficult to make due to their complex interrelationships. For another, because many of the intellectual movements of this period had their antecedents in the eighteenth and early nineteenth centuries it is necessary, in order to discuss the intellectual character of the period, to also discuss the earlier periods in which these traditions had their origins.

I begin the survey with the utilitarians, since their philosophy and the classical economics associated with it became the subject of criticism of both Continental positivists and the German historical school. This is not to say, of course, that Comtian positivism and the German historical school arose simply as movements in protest of utilitarianism, for in all likelihood they would have arisen regardless of whether utilitarianism had ever existed. However, the fact is that the philosophy of Comte and the views of the German historical school were in some respects anti-utilitarian, both in their social philosophies and in their philosophies of science.

English utilitarianism was a product of the eighteenth century that increased in influence in the early part of the nineteenth century. The intellectual leaders of the movement were Jeremy Bentham and James Mill.[42] According to Schumpeter, utilitarianism was a "philosophy of life" which fit the rationalism associated with English liberalism.[43] I

41. The issues mentioned above will be discussed in detail in the chapters following. My purpose at present is to relate these issues to the important intellectual traditions of the period.

42. I can here only refer to some of the works of these authors: Jeremy Bentham, *An Introduction to the Principles of Morals and Legislation* (1st ed. 1789; 2nd ed.; Oxford: Clarendon, 1876); James Mill, "Essay on Government," *Encyclopedia Brittanica* (suppl., 1823).

43. Joseph Schumpeter, *History of Economic Analysis* (New York: Oxford University Press, 1954), p. 408.

need only mention here that utilitarianism had a *rationalistic* conception of individual behavior and of social institutions.[44] This rationalistic conception further led to a mechanistic view of society that ascribed a degree of "regularity" to economic and social relationships. Utilitarianism was also *individualistic* in that it maintained that the common good of the society could be identified with the total "happiness" of individuals summed up to a social total. This individualistic view yielded the normative principle: the greatest happiness for the greatest number of individuals. This principle became identified with the name of Bentham. An important implication of the individualistic orientation of the utilitarians was that it caused them to separate the social whole into individual units for the purpose of analysis. This tendency became known as atomism. We shall see below that the utilitarian mechanistic-atomistic conception of society was severely attacked in Germany.

The utilitarian movement became associated with classical economics, although the degree of its influence upon classical doctrine is open to some question.[45] Some of the general policies of classical economics—such as free trade, for example—did link up with utilitarianism.[46] Other classical policies seemed to be neutral toward any philosophy. J. S. Mill did not accept utilitarianism without qualification, and it is not clear whether his thoughts represented a corrective improvement or an explicit rejection of the views of his father, James Mill. Schumpeter maintains that J. S. Mill grew to realize that utilitarian rationality was quite inadequate beyond a limited range of problems, essentially economic.[47] Whatever may be the case, J. S. Mill's "sophisticated" type of utilitarianism became established at Cambridge through his influence. Later, Jevons and Edgeworth acquiesced to the alliance betwen utilitarianism and economics, so

44. Perhaps the protean word "rationalism" needs some clarification at this point, although it will be discussed in detail in Chapter V. For the purposes of this study only three distinctions are required: (1) the belief that rational procedures are applicable to the study of social phenomena (whether or not such phenomena are logical, in the sense of a means-end criterion, from the point of view of the observer); (2) the belief that the behavior of individuals and society possesses an *inherent* logical consistency or order; (3) the belief that this rational order exists only in reason, and that reason should be asserted against a deviating reality. All three aspects apply to the utilitarians.

45. See Schumpeter, for a discussion of the relationship of utilitarianism to classical economics (*History*, p. 408).

46. The classical doctrine of real income equality as a goal also stemmed from utilitarianism.

47. Schumpeter, *History*, p. 408.

that they developed their marginal analysis within the framework of the utility postulate.[48]

Because German historical economists were of a different bent from the English economists, theoretical economics never became firmly entrenched in Germany. Like the English, many Germans were empiricists,[49] but they doubted that the conception of "laws" could be applied to the social sciences. The Germans felt that "atomism"—the isolation of particular social facts—had no place in the social sciences. One of the basic reasons for the German "organicism," i.e., the reluctance to break down analytically the concrete whole, had to do with the German concept of social reality. Social phenomena, according to this concept, could only be interpreted through their historical facets—economic, ethical, legal, cultural, etc. Nevertheless, the Germans did not oppose the use of analytical theory in the physical sciences. Thus, in calling attention to the distinction between the methods of the physical sciences and those of the social sciences, the German economists were merely reflecting the views of a broader intellectual tradition that was firmly established in Germany—the German idealistic philosophy. This tradition merits some comment, since it lies at the root of many of the methodological views of the German historians.

The German idealistic tradition, like other intellectual traditions, is very complex, and I cannot pretend to render an exhaustive survey or even an outline. Instead, I shall be content with selecting a few major strands particularly relevant to the problem of this study.

Although the influence of Kant was greatly felt in Germany, as well as internationally, the degree to which he directly influenced the German economists is subject to speculation. However, as we shall soon see, his indirect influence is certainly indisputable. For the purposes of this study, the importance of Kant's idealism is found in his dichotomy between noumena and phenomena. Noumena, to Kant, are objects that are conceived by reason and are consequently thinkable but not knowable by the senses. Phenomena are objects of experience in space and time. For Kant, "Practical Reason" fell into the noumenal sphere. This meant that man could not be entirely handled by the sciences of the phenomenal world (natural sciences) nor by the analytical generalizations characteristic of such sciences.[50] Kant did not en-

48. This also implied an acceptance of the utilitarians' interpersonal comparisons of utility.

49. Here I have the historical empiricists in mind (see pp. 19-20 below).

50. For a survey of German idealistic philosophy see: A. C. Ewing (ed.), *The Idealistic Tradition* (Glencoe, Ill.: The Free Press, 1957).

tirely remove man from scientific investigation, although he believed that man's dignity as a rational noumenal being was inaccessible to empirical investigation. Kant simply saw that man should be regarded from two different standpoints. Empirical man participated in the physical world, and hence he was subject to the laws of the phenomenal world. So regarded, man and his actions could be investigated by the methods of science, e.g., by causal laws. But Kant argued that man, as a responsible moral agent, was free and thus beyond causality in the natural sense. Therefore, in Kant's eyes, knowledge of the noumenal aspect of man's life could only be obtained by speculative methods of philosophy. The Kantian dichotomy between noumena and phenomena resulted in a scientific dualism drawing a line between the natural sciences and the science of "culture" or of mind (*Geist*).

Kant divided the worlds of *fact* and *value* in a rather absolute way. Although his scheme of dualism was further modified by his Romantic heirs (the phenomenal world was not only made relative to, but practically absorbed by, the ideal world), his division was accepted by many philosophers and scientists. The division was convenient since it allowed for a social science without any real interest in religion and morals. I shall show in the following chapter that, in his views on ethical neutrality, Pareto implicitly accepted the dichotomy of fact and value.

By Hegel's time, attempts were being made to put the world of fact and value together again. Discounting Hegel's abortive attempt to apply speculative methods of philosophy to the study of (physical) phenomena,[51] he did contribute greatly to German social thought. He was the progenitor of evolutionary, organistic, dialectical, teleological thought about human society.[52] Hegel's idealism was a source of organicism, as opposed to utilitarian "atomism."

Two important methodological views developed in Germany in keeping with the Kantian dichotomy: (1) resistance to the reduction of facts of human society to the terms of the physical world; (2) the objection to general analytical theory as a method of acquiring knowledge of human society. General theorizing being unpopular, two other courses were utilized—historical empiricism and the philosophy of history. Historical empiricism focused on the concrete histori-

51. Georg Wilhelm Friedrich Hegel, *Die Naturphilosophie* (Part II of the *System der Philosophie*, and Vol. IX [1929] of *Sämtliche Werke*, 20 vols.; Stuttgart: F. Frommann, 1927-1930). See also: Ewing, *Idealistic Tradition*, pp. 85-109.
52. These will be discussed in the course of the survey.

cal uniqueness of all human things. History was thought to be the indispensable method of acquiring knowledge, and this course gave rise to "historicism." The Hegelian branch took the second course—the philosophy of history. This branch favored the interpretation of human behavior in terms of a "spirit" (*Geist*). Historical attention became focused on the *Geist*, which constituted the unifying concept with which to arrange human activities. According to Parsons, Hegel viewed human history as a "process of objectification" of a unique *Weltgeist*.[53] The influence of historical empiricism and the philosophy of history was reflected in the main trend of German social thought. This trend placed emphasis on historically unique cultural systems and the tendency to treat all empirical data in relation to such systems. This unifying concept became a unique *Geist*—a specific cultural totality, clearly distinct from others, rather than analytical "laws." The philosophy-of-history branch of German social thought laid great stress on the relativity of cultural systems. Schmoller, for example, held that the principles embodied in the system of classical economics were not universal, but rather an expression of a *Geist* characterized by liberalism, individualism, commercialism, and *Manchestertum*. In his eyes the usefulness of the classical system was limited to the social circumstances identified by these characteristics only.

The repudiation of general analytical concepts and the corresponding emphasis on organic totality forced the German economists into methodologically dubious paths. These paths will be discussed in detail in a later chapter. It need only be mentioned here that recognition of "intuition" as a source of knowledge was attacked not only by Pareto, but also by Weber, a later member of the German historical tradition. Both writers came close to the utilitarians in their advocacy of theoretical generalizations as a source of scientific knowledge.

Schumpeter gives some of the essential points of view which resulted from detailed historical research, and which the historical school helped to establish.[54] Although I shall go into the views of the individual members of the "historical school" in detail in later chapters, Schumpeter's outline serves as a useful introduction at this point. One German point of view was that of "relativity."[55] A specific example of the relativistic view was given above in Schmoller's vision of classical economics, the principles of which, he argued, applied only

53. Parsons, *Structure*, p. 478.
54. Joseph Schumpeter, *Economic Doctrine and Method*, trans. R. Aris (London: George Allen and Unwin, 1954), pp. 175-80.
55. *Ibid.*, p. 176.

to limited social circumstances. A second point of view, which the historical school helped to establish, was that of "the unity of social life and of the inseparable correlation between the elements."[56] I have already touched upon this above. Essentially, it was argued that social phenomena were capable of interpretation only in all their historical facets, and hence that "social reality" did not permit "isolation" of particular facts.

A third point of view, also associated with the historical school, was that of "anti-rationalism."[57] We shall see later that the Germans were critical of the utilitarian ideal of rational behavior on normative as well as on methodological grounds. Some members rejected the utilitarian postulate of rational behavior as a norm. Others argued that social phenomena could not be "rationalized" as could physical phenomena because human behavior involved an element of "free will" that was lacking in physical phenomena. Hence human behavior was not subject to the "regularities" of physical phenomena, thus denying the valid use of "laws." A fourth point of view was "interest in individual correlations."[58] This view focused attention, as has been mentioned, on the concrete individuality and historical uniqueness of all things human. Human history never repeated itself, so that each historical epoch was a unique and individual thing to be treated only as such. The idea of concrete individuality and historical uniqueness was so strongly entrenched in German thought that even Weber, who disagreed with his predecessors on many other views mentioned here, held firmly to it.

A fifth view identifiable with the historical school was that of "organicism."[59] The term "organicism" had several interpretations. It was used merely as a kind of analogy between the social body and the physical body. It was also used to mean that the "total is something greater than the sum of its parts," so that the whole cannot be split up into individual parts for analysis without loss of "reality." Another use of the term stressed the close mutual dependency of categories of social phenomena, although recognizing their "independence" for specialized study.

Finally, the historical economists believed that theories of "evolution"[60] were bound to make greater use of historical material. This view was never seriously challenged by Pareto, who looked upon his-

56. *Ibid.*
57. *Ibid.*, p. 177.
58. *Ibid.*, p. 178.
59. *Ibid.*, p. 179.
60. *Ibid.*, p. 178.

tory as an indispensable tool for sociology. It should be pointed out that Schumpeter's characterization of the German historical school's views is not entirely representative of all the German economists associated with that group. Some members stressed certain views while ignoring others. In later chapters I shall focus attention on the individuals connected with each view.

German idealistic philosophy never ruled unchallenged on the Continent. Comte's positivism exerted a powerful influence upon the social sciences, and gathered considerable influence as the nineteenth century wore on. Comte's philosophy represented a reaction to speculative philosophy. He looked upon his "positive" philosophy as an advancement in intellectual evolution. On the other hand, he was also critical of the atomistic orientations of the utilitarians. The importance of Comte's positivism is that it represented a third major intellectual tradition, which influenced trends in scientific thought. Pareto was greatly influenced by Comte's scientific doctrines—his philosophy of science—and for this reason I shall devote particular attention to the important parts of Comte's philosophy.

Comte's philosophy was more than a philosophy of science; it was also a social philosophy. He saw the political and social unrest in Europe as anarchy arising from the anarchy of ideas:

I believe that I can exactly sum up all the observations made upon the present condition of society by simply saying that the present intellectual anarchy depends, at bottom, *on the simultaneous employment of three philosophies radically incompatible: the theological, the metaphysical, and the positive.* It is a clear fact, that if any of those three philosophies really obtained a universal and complete preponderance, there would be a determinant social order, whereas our especial evil consists in the absence of all true organization whatsoever.[61]

Regardless of the merits or lack of merits of Comte's observations in the above citation, he did create a philosophy of science for a new social faith. His *aim* was a social doctine; his means were scientific doctrines.[62]

Comte's positive philosophy involved three intitial conceptions. The first of these was that all sciences—physical and social—as branches of one Science were to be investigated by one and the same

61. Auguste Comte, *Cours de philosophie positive* (6 vols.; Paris: Schleicher, 1830), I, 57.

62. The following are recommended as studies of various aspects of Comte's philosophy: Ernst Cassirer, *The Problem of Knowledge* (New York: Yale University Press, 1950), pp. 243-55; G. H. Lewes, *Comte's Philosophy of the Sciences* (London: George Bell and Sons, 1904); John Watson, *Comte, Mill and Spencer* (Glasgow: James Maclehose and Sons, 1895), pp. 21-42.

method. Here we find a denial of the Kantian dichotomy, with no logical distinction being made between the physical sciences and the science of "culture."

His second initial conception was that there were three phases of intellectual evolution, for the individual as well as for the mass: the theological (supernatural), the metaphysical (speculative philosophy), and the positive (science). In the *supernatural* phase the mind seeks *causes;* it aspires to know the *essences* of things. It regards all effects as the products of supernatural agents. In the *metaphysical* phase, a modification takes place; the supernatural agents are set aside for abstract forces or "entities," supposedly inherent in various substances and capable of engendering phenomena. In the *positive* phase, the mind, convinced of the futility of all inquiry into causes and essences, restricts itself to the observation and classification of phenomena and to the discovery of the invariable relationships that things bear to each other—in a word, to the discovery of *laws* of phenomena.

The third conception was the classification of the sciences co-ordinated by the principle of commencing with the study of the simplest phenomena and proceeding successively to the most complex, thus arranging the sciences according to their dependence upon each other. He tried to arrange all scientific knowledge into a hierarchy of sciences, beginning with mathematics, then astronomy, physics, chemistry, biology, and "sociology" (the science of society). He proceeded to furnish the elements important to each science and their relations to the adjoining sciences.

Comte distinguished between the non-evolutionary phenomena, which took the form of laws and acted and reacted upon each other, and the evolutionary phenomena, which were associated with social change. Non-evolutionary phenomena formed the static elements in the system which produced an equilibrating order of society. Such phenomena were essentially human "instincts." Evolutionary phenomena were the dynamic elements, essentially *intellectual.* According to Comte, intellectual evolution was the predominating principle in social evolution. Intellectual evolution involved, as shown above, a progression from the theological to the metaphysical to the positive state of mind.

Comte saw the establishment of positive philosophy as the presiding and influencing agent in the general reconstruction of the system of education. Education, or, more precisely, positive education, was to be the harmonizing spirit of the age, suited to the wants of modern civilization.

Comte was also concerned with the increasing specialization taking place in the physical sciences, which, he believed, caused a fragmentation of knowledge. He saw in his sociology a remedy for the problem of fragmentation of knowledge, in that "positive sociology" was to be a "synthesis" binding together all positive knowledge. The lower sciences in the hierarchy were to be "analytical," with each step upward towards "sociology" being also a step towards the ultimate "synthesis" of positive knowledge.

Comte's methodology involved the observation of historical facts and the building of a science of society from generalizations suggested by these facts. However, he had the mistaken impression that physical science methods, which he thought he was using, involved the derivation of generalizations from observed historical facts without the intervention of theory in any form during the process. He didn't seem to realize that physical science does not accept unanalyzed fact, but that the selection of facts in itself implies theorizing.

H. T. Buckle attempted to reduce history to a positive science in the Comtian sense of the term, but he was swayed by pure speculation.[63] Herbert Spencer aimed at the same goals as Comte, because he was looking for a substitute for metaphysical speculation and a general body of thought to rationalize specialized research. Contrary to Comte, he emphasized the irrational elements in society.[64]

Let us now contrast the methodological aspects of the intellectual movements discussed above. English utilitarianism was attacked on several grounds. In the first place, its social philosophy—that of individual rationalism together with the principle of "the greatest happiness for the greatest number," and the creeds to which these gave rise—was attacked, especially by the German economists. Some of the German writers doubted that the rational procedures of science were applicable to the study of social phenomena. Others denied that individuals, and especially society, possessed an *inherent* logical consistency. Also, the German economists' schemes for social reform were not compatible with the *laissez faire* doctrines of the English economists. Hence, German writers attacked utilitarian rationalism for methodological as well as normative reasons.[65] Comte, on the other hand, adopted the concept of rational behavior as the cornerstone of his positive science.

---

63. Henry T. Buckle, *History of Civilization in England* (3 vols.; London: Parker & Son, 1901).

64. Cf. Herbert Spencer, *The Classification of the Sciences* (New York: Appleton, 1864); *Principles of Sociology* (New York: Appleton, 1896).

65. The specific writers and their views will be discussed in later chapters.

The German historical economists tended to link utilitarianism with "classical" economics. This led them to condemn English economic theory as well. The wholesale condemnation of English economic theory was not justifiable. As we shall see later, in economic analysis, which works with rational schemata, utility postulates (though superfluous) do no harm. With respect to economic sociology, the German historical economists had a better case in condemning classical economics, for the rationalistic conception of individual behavior within the broader scope of sociology was open to doubt, both as a theoretical assumption and as a normative principle.[66]

We have seen above that the German economists made a distinction between the methodology of the physical sciences and that of the social sciences. They accused the English economic theorists of adopting physical science's methods—the isolation of particular facts that form the basis for specialized disciplines—methods which were not valid, according to the Kantian tradition. Comte, of course, was even more explicit than the English economists in his intention of adopting the methods of "positive" science. In his eyes all sciences, both physical and social, were to be investigated by the same method. The German economists were at odds with both the English economic theorists and the Comtian positivists on the question of the methodology of the physical and social sciences.

Both the German economists and Comte attacked classical economics on empirical grounds. The Germans argued that English economic theory was speculative and unrealistic. Comte accused the "classic" economists of unscientific speculation. However, he did not mean what the economists of the historical school had in mind, for Comte was perfectly willing to use generalizations in the form of "laws." He differed with the classical economists, particularly with J. S. Mill, in that Comte believed, as I have explained above, that generalizations from observed historical facts could be derived without theory. J. S. Mill realized Comte's error, arguing that the selection of facts in itself implies theorizing.[67] Finally, to compound the confusion, Comte attacked German metaphysics as speculative and unscientific. He argued that the German philosophers were either unable or unwilling to give to the world a philosophy of science that rationalized the analytical procedures used by scientists. Hegel's abortive attempt certainly was not a rationalization of the procedures used

66. Again I must postpone a detailed discussion of the views until later chapters.
67. Cf. Watson, *Comte, Mill and Spencer*, p. 86; Schumpeter, *History*, p. 452.

by scientists, but a substitute for science which used speculative methods of philosophy to "explain" physical phenomena.

Continuing with the historical sketch, we come to Marx. Marx represented another major orientation in scientific methodology. He admitted that his philosophy was strongly influenced by Hegel; nevertheless, he claimed that his positive research into the facts of capitalistic society was non-Hegelian. There appears to be some truth to Marx's claim, since his vision of the capitalist process can be traced to Ricardo.[68]

However, there are similarities in the schemata of Marx and Hegel. Marx, like Hegel, conceived of the development of mankind as a single process towards a determinate goal. Also like Hegel, he thought of the process not as a continuous single line with quantitative increases, but as dialectical. That is, the continuous process was characterized by stages forming well-marked systems distinct from others in organization, and arising in direct conflict with immediate predecessors in the series. For Marx, the "mode of production" determined the class structure that characterized each social system. The capitalistic system was merely one such system in the process of evolution subsumed under the generalized unifying principle of the productive process.

According to Parsons, Marx differed from Hegel with respect to the dynamic element in the evolutionary process.[69] Hegel's dynamic forces of history were to be found in the self-development of a *Geist,* while for Marx they were to be found in men's class "interests." The difference between Hegelian idealism and Marxian materialism lies in the distinction between the dynamic elements of both authors' systems. For Marx, the conditions of production were the fundamental determinants of social structure, which in turn determined individuals' ways of looking at reality. Here we find a crucial departure from Comte regarding the individual's perception of reality. Comte made no explicit distinction between the experiences of various classes of individuals. For him, positive education was to be the harmonizing spirit of the age, suited to the wants of modern civilization. In the Marxian schema the nature of the experiences of different classes was all-important. The experiences of the capitalists and proletarians were fundamentally different. The experience of each class molded the class outlook on social reality. Members of a class shared the same outlook not only because they had the same interests, but because

68. Cf. Schumpeter, *History,* p. 414, for a discussion of Marx's and Ricardo's systems.
69. Parsons, *Structure,* p. 485.

they shared the same experiences. Hence the *materialistic* interpretation of history was not necessarily the *economic* interpretation of history.

Karl Popper discusses Marx's process of determination, which I shall only outline at this point: (1) social systems or class systems change with the conditions of production; (2) class relations characteristic of social systems are independent of the individual's will; (3) although the social system has a kind of logic of its own, it works blindly, not rationally; (4) individuals are unable to foresee the repercussions of their actions; (5) the social system influences the pattern of their behavior.[70]

One implication of Marx's process of determination is that institutions, morals, and ideas (including scientific opinions) are determined by class position or, more generally, by the social or historical situation. Man is not the master of his own fate. Hence, the doctrine of class interests is opposed to rationalism. In Marx's sociology of knowledge, the interest-bound nature of ideas precludes the possibility of a rational or even an "objective" social science.

One important implication of the sociology of knowledge, at least for my purposes, is that all scientific thought or knowledge is "condition" by the social (or psychological) position of the observer. Hence, the idea of scientific "objectivity" is meaningless.[71] If the idea of "scientific objectivity" rested upon the notion of the individual scientist's impartiality *alone,* then it would seem true that the concept of "scientific objectivity" is meaningless in the light of the sociology of knowledge. However, an ethically neutral state of mind is not the only criterion for scientific objectivity. We shall see in a later chapter that both Pareto and Weber argued that the subjective (immediate) experience of an individual scientist, no matter what the source, must be checked by reference to a logically consistent system of concepts, if "intuitional" judgments are to be avoided. Hence, through the critical proof of scientific theory, subjective experience is "objectified." Also, Pareto and Weber considered the free interaction and criticism of ideas within the scientific community to be an extremely important aspect of objective science.

70. Karl Popper, *The Open Society and Its Enemies* (Princeton, N. J.: Princeton University Press, 1950), pp. 304-8. Popper argues that Marx was not as much of a materialist as is often attributed to him. He believes that Marx's writings indicated a leaning towards a dualism of the body (materialism) and the mind (idealism) (p. 295).

71. See Popper, *Open Society,* chap. xxiii, for an interpretation of K. Mannheim's and M. Scheler's sociology of knowledge. Individual authors will be discussed in a later chapter.

The value of the sociology of knowledge lies in making the social scientists aware of the social forces and "ideologies" that influence them, not in its alleged denial of the possibility of a social science. This problem will receive close attention in the following chapter.[72]

The intellectual traditions discussed above represent the main currents of the intellectual thought of Pareto's time, at least as far as methodology is concerned. There were also minor currents during this period, which—with one exception—never really developed into full-scale intellectual movements. These deserve mention because Pareto's works seem to reflect their influence.

Romanticism, the exception among these minor currents of the eighteenth century, did develop into a full-fledged intellectual movement during the period under consideration. From a methodological viewpoint, the importance of the movement was in its anti-rationalistic orientations and its emphasis on historical research. Romanticism was not a philosophy, a social creed,[73] or a political or economic system, as were the movements I discussed above. Romanticism was essentially a literary fashion linked with certain attitudes towards life and art. The romanticists were *literati* who also roamed the fields of philosophy and social science. Below the surface was a revolt against rationalism and cold reason. Romanticism opposed rational individualism and emphasized extra-rational universalism. The romantic conception of liberty and democracy was not that of Bentham and the utilitarians, but rather what liberty and democracy meant to people as they are, think, and feel—rational or not. The romantic writers also revived interest in historical research preceding the eighteenth century. The movement was strongly Catholic. It has been identified with political reaction, which was anti-capitalist and, hence, anti-development.[74]

72. Paul Kecskemeti, who edited Karl Mannheim, *Essays on the Sociology of Knowledge* (New York: Oxford University Press, 1952), argues that Mannheim believed that in spite of the inescapability of certain relativist conclusions, genuine knowledge of historical and social phenomena was possible. According to Mannheim, "participation in the social process, which renders one's perspective partial and biased, also enables one to discover truth of deep human import" (p. 1). Later, Mannheim incorporated psychological elements into his basic idea of social structure. He turned to Freudian psychology in order to clarify some of the decisive factors in social change, especially war. See: Karl Mannheim, *Essays on Sociology and Social Psychology* (New York: Oxford University Press, 1953).

73. Mannheim believed that the conservative and romantic climate of thought in Germany could be accounted for in terms of a real struggle among concrete social groups. Cf. Mannheim, *Essays on the Sociology of Knowledge,* pp. 20-22.

74. Hegel shows a very fine comprehension of tendencies which the romantic movement had notably exemplified. Cf. Josiah Royce, "Hegel's

After the middle of the nineteenth century some minor currents of thought developed in Europe which were against liberal rationality and its concept of human "progress." Anti-democratic and antihumanitarian currents developed. The work of Nietzsche is often presented as an example of such currents. The work of Georges Sorel presents one of the best examples of an attitude that was antagonistic toward bourgeois intellectualism and which expressed contempt for parliamentary democracy and the bourgeois ideal of progress.[75] Pareto was a great admirer of Sorel.

This ends the survey of the intellectual character of the period. It is by no means complete, but an attempt towards completeness would involve a major work.

Phenomenology of Mind," *Lectures on Modern Idealism* (New Haven: Yale University Press, 1919).

75. Georges Sorel, *Réflexions sur la violence* (Paris: Riviere, 1908).

III Ethical Neutrality Requirement

Each of the intellectual traditions presented in the preceding chapter expounded a set of philosophical principles for the scientific investigation of human society. Such principles constitute a philosophy of science. Comte's philosophy of science involved the recognition of physical science methods as valid sources of the scientific knowledge of human society. The main concern of this section will be with the Comtian sense of the term "scientific," which distinguishes the procedures of "positive" science from theological and metaphysical principles. My purpose in introducing Comte at this point is to establish the influence of Comte upon Pareto and, in turn, to see in what ways Pareto's views represent a departure from Comte's philosophy. Once Pareto's intellectual orientation has been determined, what follows in this chapter can be presented with little difficulty.

Pareto's intellectual orientation has been the subject of some confusion in the secondary sources. Millikan has compared Pareto to Bacon, seeing a similarity in their "somewhat naive empiricism."[1] John Harrington believes that "Newton can be said to have furnished inspiration for Pareto's methodology."[2] Werner Stark seems unable to decide just where Pareto's methodology and intellectual orientations belong. He links Pareto to Plato,[3] Weber,[4] and Nietzsche,[5] in one of his works. Later he sees an affinity between the "rationalistic" views

1. Max Millikan, "Pareto's Sociology," *Econometrica*, IV (Dec., 1936), 324.
2. John Harrington, "Vilfredo Pareto," *Social Theorists* ed. C. Mihanovich (Milwaukee: Bruce Publishing Co., 1953), p. 175.
3. Werner Stark, *The Sociology of Knowledge* (Glencoe, Ill.: The Free Press, 1958), p. 51.
4. *Ibid.,* p. 193.
5. *Ibid.,* p. 322.

of Kant and Pareto.[6] Finally, in a recent article he concludes that "Pareto was simply the last of the many 'Newtons of the Moral World.' "[7] Schumpeter detects a closeness in the views (as well as a physical resemblance) of Sorel and Pareto.[8] Pantaleoni tells us that Pareto was influenced by Comte quite early in his intellectual development.[9] More recently Bobbio has concluded that "Pareto's philosophical and methodological leanings undoubtedly derive from Comte."[10]

The observations of Pantaleoni and Bobbio appear to be most valid. There is a striking similarity between Pareto's views on "logico-experimental" science and Comte's views on "positive" science. "Logico-experimental" science, as defined by Pareto, deals with principles that have their origin in "observation" and "experience," in contradistinction to the "non-logico-experimental" principles of theology and metaphysics.[11] The concepts embodied in these terms seem to have as their origin Comte's views as expressed in the *Cours de philosophie positive,* from which Pareto quoted (brackets contain Pareto's comments):

"I use the term 'philosophy' in the acceptation given it by the ancients, and specifically Aristotle, as designating the general system of human concepts. Appending to it the word 'positive,' I give notice that I am envisaging the special manner of philosophizing that lies in viewing theories of whatever order as purposing to coordinate observed facts. [That, really, would be the experimental method.] In the positive stage, the human mind comes to recognize the impossibility of obtaining absolute concepts. It abandons the quest for the origin and destiny of the universe and for knowledge of the inner causes of phenomena, and tries merely to discover by the use of reasoning and observation combined

6. Werner Stark, *The Fundamental Forms of Social Thought* (London: Routledge & Kegan Paul, 1962), p. 130.
7. Werner Stark, "In Search of the True Pareto," *British Journal of Sociology,* XIV (June, 1963), 107.
8. Joseph Schumpeter, *History of Economic Analysis,* (New York: Oxford University Press, 1954), p. 775.
9. Maffeo Pantaleoni, "Vilfredo Pareto," *Economic Journal,* XXXIII (Sept., 1923), 589.
10. Norberto Bobbio, "Introduction to Pareto's Sociology," *Banca Nazional del Lavoro, Quarterly Review,* No. 69 (June, 1964), p. 194.
11. In Italian, the word *esperienza* contains the meaning of "experiment" as well as "experience." The word "experience" is so used in the translation of the *Trattato* by Arthur Livingston. Livingston's translation of *esperienza* to the English "experimental" is a cause for confusion since it conveys the impression that Pareto believed that all science was experimental. Of course, this is not correct. A better term would be "logico-observational." One reason I compare Pareto's views with those of Comte in this section is to show that Pareto's conception of science is exactly the same as Comte's "positive" science, with a few important exceptions discussed in the text.

their actual laws, in other words, their invariable relations of succession and likeness." And that again would be a definition of the logico-experimental method.[12]

In the above citation, Pareto's principles of "experimental" science are exactly the same as those of Comte's "positive" science. The two authors differed sharply, however, in their classification of "non-logico-experimental" (Pareto) and "non-positive" (Comte) sciences. Comte's classification of "non-positive" science included theological and metaphysical principles; Pareto added "pseudo-experimental" principles to "theological" and "metaphysical" principles as examples of "non-logico-experimental" science. Before going on to discuss Pareto's "pseudo-experimental" designation, let us first compare the similarities between the views of Pareto and Comte on "theological" and "metaphysical" principles.

For Pareto, "theological" principles were those principles that found their criteria of truth in Holy Writ, the will of a Deity, divine revelation, etc.[13] Spinoza's approach was cited as an illustration by Pareto:

Spinoza is looking for a "first and general cause" for motion (blessed was he who knew what that meant!). He observes that we must admit nothing we cannot clearly and distinctly perceive: "and since *we* [Pareto's italics] clearly and distinctly perceive no other cause except God—that is to say, the Creator of matter—it becomes manifest that no general cause is to be admitted except God." But who, pray, are the people designated by the pronoun "we"? Assuredly not all human beings—for the reasons already given: and since not all, how is one to go about selecting the few, the many, who are to be blessed by inclusion among the "we," and separating them from the reprobates who are to be left in the outer darkness? Spinoza "clearly and distinctly" sees God as the "cause" of motion—and what luck! But there are plenty of people who only do not "clearly and distinctly" see God as the "cause" of motion, but who do not even know what "God" or "matter" can possibly be.[14]

The "non-experimental" character of these principles is quite clear, and Pareto did not dwell upon them to any great extent.[15]

12. Vilfredo Pareto, *The Mind and Society,* trans. and ed. A. Livingston (4 vols.; New York: Harcourt, Brace and Co., 1935), III, sec. 1537 n. 1, pp. 984-85. Reference is to Auguste Comte, *Cours de philosophie positive* (6 vols.; Paris: Schleicher, 1830), I, xiii and 3.

13. Pareto, *Mind and Society,* I, sec. 67, p. 32.

14. *Ibid.,* sec. 601, pp. 362-63. Pareto could hardly be praised for his understanding of the spirit of Spinoza's system. What is important for my purpose is that Pareto, like Comte, did not consider theological principles an important source of scientific knowledge.

15. However, the existence of theological principles is important as data for

On the other hand, "metaphysical" principles were often used by metaphysicians in the name of "science." Metaphysicians generally gave the name of "science" to the knowledge of the "essences" of things. As far as Pareto (and Comte) were concerned, "experimental" science not only refrained from dealing with "essences," it did not even know the meaning of that term. The postulates used in metaphysical propositions contained no observable implications.[16] Since these propositions contained no observable implications, i.e., were outside of "objective experience," they could only be accepted or rejected on the basis of individual sentiments.[17] Under these circumstances, "proofs" of such propositions amounted to nothing more than exhortations.

It seems that Pareto's criticisms of metaphysical principles were valid from a strictly scientific viewpoint. Metaphysical principles are not altered on the basis of experience, and they usually yield moral rather than factual implications. Scientific postulates, on the contrary, are mere hypotheses, which endure only so long as their deduced consequences correspond to concrete facts. The standard of truth for "experimental" science lies within "experience." The proof of such propositions lies in observation, experience, and the logical inferences

---

the study of sociological phenomena. This aspect Pareto considers to be very important.

16. Pareto, *Mind and Society*, I, secs. 28, 56, pp. 18, 27.

17. Pareto distinguishes between "objective" and "subjective" experience and also between "objective" and "subjective" reality (this distinction will be discussed in detail in Chapter V). But he refuses to go beyond that distinction and treat the philosophical problem of the "reality of the external world": "When we assert that to know the properties of sulphuric anhydride one must appeal to experience and not, as Hegelian metaphysics would have it, to the 'concept' of sulphur or even of oxygen, we are not in the least intending to set an external world over against an internal world, and objective reality over a subjective reality. We can state the same proposition in a jargon that recognizes the 'existence' of nothing but thought. We can say, that is, to get the concept of sulphuric anhydride, it is not enough to have the mere concepts of sulphur and oxygen and meditate upon them. We could do that for century on century without getting the concepts supplied by chemical experiment. The ancient philosophers thought that they could replace observation and experience in just that way, but they were entirely wrong. Chemistry is learned in laboratories and not by philosophical meditations, even of the Hegelian brand. To get the concept, or concepts, of sulphuric anhydride we must first have many concepts acquired through the concept otherwise known as experience—burning sulphur in oxygen or in air, and collecting the concept of sulphuric anhydride in the concept of a glass container—finally bringing all such concepts together to get the concept of the properties of sulphuric anhydride. But such a jargon would be prolix, tedious, ridiculous; and just to avoid it we use the terms 'subjective' and 'objective.' For the logico-experimental purposes we have in view no other terms are required" (*Ibid.*, sec. 95, pp. 50-51).

from observation and theory.[18] Experimental science looks for what is.[19]

In his observations regarding the distinction between "experimental" principles and theological and metaphysical principles, Pareto was merely repeating the thoughts of Comte. However, he did add to Comte's classification by introducing the concept of "pseudo-experimental" principles. "Pseudo-experimental" principles occurred with the attempt to give some empirical substantiation to theology and metaphysics:

Theology and metaphysics do not wholly disdain experience, provided it be their servant. They take great pride in showing that their pseudo-experimental inferences are verified by the facts, but the believer and the metaphysicist already know, prior to any experimental investigation, that the verification would turn out wonderfully, since a "higher principle would never permit it to do otherwise." In their explorations in the realm beyond experience they satisfy a hankering that is active and even tyrannical in many people for knowing not only what has been and is, but also what ought or must necessarily be; and, meantime, in professing to have taken experience into account—whether well or badly matters a little—they escape the opprobrium of going counter to the scientific current, or even to plain good sense. But the facts that they take into account are facts selected for a definite purpose, and serving no other purpose than to justify a theory preconceived—not that it needs any justification, but just for good measure! The part assigned to experience may now be insignificant, then again very considerable; but large or small, it is always within those limits and under those conditions. The doctrines of Comte and Spencer are types of this class.[20]

Notice that in the above citation Pareto refers to the doctrines of Comte and Spencer as examples of "pseudo-experimental" princi-

18. *Ibid.,* sec. 56, p. 27. Pareto realized that the criteria for "testing" metaphysical and "logico-experimental" principles were entirely different. Metaphysics recognized a knowledge of "essences" as a valid source of scientific knowledge. The transformation of "essences" into operationally meaningful propositions was a fundamental difficulty which metaphysicians could not overcome. I have already mentioned Hegel's ineffectual attempt to use speculative methods of philosophy in order to arrive at the same conclusions the physical sciences had arrived at through the use of their own methods (i.e., "logico-experimental," to use a Paretian term). I should also point out that Pareto's criticism of metaphysics makes it clear that he was only thinking of a limited kind of nineteenth-century German metaphysics (e.g., Hegel's works).

19. *Ibid.* The term "what is" may be interpreted as applying either to descriptive studies of the state of society or to studies of the nature of society (i.e., to what laws, regularities, relations, etc., society is subjected). Comte and Pareto used the term in the latter sense.

20. *Ibid.,* sec. 613, pp. 369-70.

ples. This is merely one of many attacks leveled against Comte and Spencer. Pareto's continuous bombasts against Comte may be one reason why some of the writers mentioned above failed to detect the influence of Comte upon Pareto's methodology. In the *Systèmes socialistes* Pareto dwelt at length and in a caustic spirit on Comte's positive philosophy. Finally, in the *Trattato,* he dismissed Comte's philosophy as an evolutionary regression from the "experimental" to the "metaphysical" to the "theological."[21]

Pareto had also counted Spencer among his favorite authors. Later, in the *Systèmes socialistes,* he insinuated that Spencer, too, like J. S. Mill, began with a critique of Comte and ended by embracing a kind of metaphysical religion.[22]

In the *Trattato* both of Pareto's old idols were shattered. Pareto no longer saw any methodological differences between the doctrines of Comte and Spencer. Their alleged scientific systems were said to be "different religions, but even so . . . always religions."[23] In other words, Comte and Spencer did not end where they began. Some writers on Pareto detect, in his apparent change of methodological orientation, an inconsistent thinker who first expounded and then attacked positivism.[24] The fact of the matter is that Pareto was critical of Comte for the latter's failure to practice what he preached. Pareto accused Comte of not being a positivist!

Was Pareto correct in his claim, or was he merely ranting about devils of his own creation? It seems that there was some substance to Pareto's claim, although he tended towards exaggeration. We have seen in the preceding chapter that Comte's expressed intention in the *Cours* was to restrict himself to the observation and classification of phenomena, and to the discovery of the invariable relations that things bear to each other. Nevertheless, there was a tendency on his part not to just "co-ordinate" the facts, as he promised, but to impose upon them certain value judgments that violated his own positivistic principles. Pareto was perhaps too sweeping in his criticism of Comte when he maintained that the whole of Comte's *Cours* might be cited as proof of his allegations: "At every forward step one meets such adjectives as 'true,' 'sane,' 'necessary,' 'inevitable,' 'irrevocable,' 'perfect,' through which Comte tries to subordinate the facts to his ideas

21. *Ibid.,* III, sec. 1537, pp. 985-86.
22. Vilfredo Pareto, *Les systèmes socialistes* (2 vols.; Paris: Giard et Brière, 1902-3), II, 197. Cf. Bobbio, *Banca Nazional del Lavoro, Quarterly Review,* No. 69, pp. 193-95, for a summary of Pareto's critique of Comte, Mill, and Spencer.
23. Pareto, *Mind and Society,* I, sec. 6, pp. 5-6.
24. See above, p. 10, for an example of Stark as such a writer.

instead of coordinating the facts and subordinating his ideas to them."[25]

One specific example that Pareto cited from Comte better supported the basis for his critique:

"This first scientific exercise of the abstract sense of evidence, i.e., of the nature of proof of harmony, however limited in scope at first, was enough to provoke an important philosophical reaction, which, for the moment favorable to metaphysical speculations only, was none the less a remote predecessor of the *inevitable* [Pareto's italics] advent of a positive philosophy by making sure of the early elimination of a theology then preponderant." In that Comte is evidently thinking of Newton and Newton's successors. But where on earth did Comte discover that the "advent" of positive philosophy was "inevitable"? If that is not a mere tautology, a way of saying that what has happened had to happen—mere determinism, in other words—it indicates that Comte is subordinating his facts to certain dogmas. He adds: "In that, the ancient unity of our mental system, which down to that time had been uniformly theological, was irrevocably broken up." But from what "coordination of facts" can Comte be inferring that such a break in the old uniformity was "irrevocable"?[26]

Thus, the scientific aspect of Comte's positivism, which was suggestive of Pareto's "logico-experimental" method, actually took on a "pseudo-experimental" form because of Comte's introduction of judgments for which no factual substance existed.

Pareto never accepted Comte's principles of intellectual evolution. It will be recalled that for Comte there were three phases of intellectual evolution—the theological, the metaphysical, and the positive. The positive phase of intellectual development was to give to mankind a "scientifically" determined society. Pareto was less optimistic. He saw Comte's positivism, at most, as a transitional stage between "theories based wholly on blind faith"—between strictly theological, metaphysical, or ethical notions—and a "definitely experimental frame of mind."[27] The chasm between the two worlds was too great to be taken in one leap, and "pseudo-experimental" principles provided the bridge. In a way, Comtian positivism was quite a step forward in the nineteenth-century development of the social sciences, since at least "experience" was being admitted. Pareto observed that once experience was admitted to the theological edifice, that portion within the experimental domain began to "crumble." However, he was not so naive as to believe that "science" had won the battle. The need to

25. Pareto, *Mind and Society,* III, sec. 1537, pp. 985-86.
26. *Ibid.,* sec. 1537 n. 2, pp. 985-86. Reference is to Comte, *Cours,* VII, 286-87.
27. Pareto, *Mind and Society,* I, sec. 615, pp. 370-71.

subordinate positive science to certain dogmas is so great in human beings that straightway a new structure of the same material is reared. That was the case with positivism, which at bottom was just one of the numerous varieties of metaphysics: "the old metaphysics fell for a brief moment, and then at once came to life again in positivisitic form."[28] Although positivism was threatening to crumble, he pessimistically thought that in its turn another metaphysical structure would be erected "because people obstinately insist on deifying a certain entity to which they have given the name of Truth."[29]

Pareto cannot be called a doctrinaire positivist since he did not accept that "new faith" which, he believed, was just another metaphysics. His skepticism prevented him from paying court to positivism (or to any other "ism," for that matter) because he doubted that individuals and society would accept and be guided exclusively by "logico-experimental" principles. In attacking the "non-experimental" principles of theology, metaphysics, and "pseudo-experimentalism" as unscientific, Pareto was not unware of their great social implications and hence their importance as sociological data to be considered in such studies. In fact, he realized that their great social utility was why such theories very often survived even when they were shown to be experimentally false.[30]

Pareto and Comte were farthest apart on the role of hypotheses as a source of scientific knowledge. Comte believed that hypotheses were unscientific theoretical speculations, which characterized the metaphysical stage of intellectual development. He especially singled out the English economists as perpetrators of unscientific theoretical speculations. In this sense Comte was anti-theoretical. I shall show in a later chapter that Pareto certainly was not anti-theoretical. In contrast to Comte, he looked upon "hypothetical abstractions" as an important source of scientific knowledge.

In summary, the scientific aspects of Comte's positivism took on a "pseudo-experimental" form due to Comte's introduction of value judgments. Perhaps Pareto's greatest departure from Comte's positivism was on the question of the role of the hypothesis in science. Finally, Pareto's skepticism prevented him from paying court to Comtian positivism, which he believed was just another metaphysics. For these reasons, Pareto's methodological views represented a de-

---

28. *Ibid.,* sec. 616, p. 371.
29. *Ibid.*
30. *Ibid.,* IV, sec. 1553, pp. 1859-60. Pareto gives great weight in his sociology to the significance of "non-experimental" principles in guiding the "non-logical" conduct of persons. This point will be covered in detail in a later chapter.

parture from the intellectual tradition that had the greatest influence upon him.

THE PROBLEM OF ETHICAL NEUTRALITY

Before going into Pareto's views on ethical neutrality, it might be useful to consider the problem in its relation to the history of economics. The problem has been stated in such ways as: "What *is* versus what *ought to be,*" or "positive versus normative theory." Regardless of how the problem is stated, the main issue, at bottom, is whether any social science can be or should be free of ethical principles. Many of the polemics that occurred in economics involved disputes over ethical principles (what ought to be) rather than "scientific" principles (what is). Very often, economic doctrine was the expression of economic, political, or social reformers attempting to "rationalize" one favored system of ethics or another. One only need read Gide and Rist, *A History of Economic Doctrines*[31] or Schumpeter's *History of Economic Analysis* to appreciate the fact that, very often, the basis for controversy among antagonistic schools of thought was ethical.

The utilitarian economists applied themselves not to what was, but to what ought to be, very often substituting ethical principles of rationalism for the objective study of facts.[32] Such procedures could be excused in the case of the early classicists, such as Adam Smith and Jean Baptiste Say, because in those days it seemed to these writers that civilization was undergoing a new birth and that knowledge and rational behavior would lead to material and intellectual development. In those circumstances the chief function of the economists was to dissipate "ignorance" by teaching and preaching the "truth." Although Malthus was not a utilitarian, in his population theories one finds a mixture of scientific research and sermonizing. Pareto himself rendered an exhaustive analysis of Malthus' theories which is unsurpassed even today. His conclusions are summarized as follows:

> The theories of Malthus give an example of the error in which one inevitably falls when one confuses theory with practice, scientific research with moral sermons. The work of Malthus is very confused and it is often very difficult to know precisely what arguments he wants to treat. In substance four parts can be distinguished in that work:

. . . .

31. Gide and Rist, *A History of Economy Doctrines,* trans. R. Richards (2nd ed.; Boston: D. C. Heath & Co., 1948).
32. See pp. 17, 24-25, above.

1. A scientific part, namely a research of the uniformity of phenomena.

. . . .

2. A descriptive and historical part in which the author wants to demonstrate the existence of the effects of two types of checks.

. . . .

3. A polemic part, in which the author wants to demonstrate that man's well-being or poor state depends almost exclusively on restricting more or less the number of births. Such part is manifestly erroneous.

. . . .

4. A preceptive part. The author has discovered the universal panacea, namely moral restraint or, if we want to express it with terms now in use he has resolved "the social question"; he sermonizes and reveals the great mystery to the people.[33]

Pareto thought that the practical implications of classical ethical and economic thought applied to England and that the generality of classical theories was open to question. Hence, he took a position very similar to that of Schmoller regarding the "relativity" of classical economics. Let us go more deeply into the matter of the "relativity" of classical doctrines, especially those of free trade.

It seemed at first that the validity of the practical aims of classical political economy (the desire to dissipate the darkness of ignorance, to defeat and abolish protection and establish free trade, and the central concern with individual freedom as a means to greater intellectual and material well-being) was confirmed by England's industrial growth during the period 1820-80. It was soon found, however, that in other countries where leagues in imitation of Cobden's came into being,[34] England's pattern of development was not even remotely duplicated. Protection became the rule. The blame for the failure of other countries to accept the doctrine of free trade was often laid on the

33. Vilfredo Pareto, *Manuale d'economia politica* (Milano: Società editrice libraria, 1906), chap. vii., secs. 89-96, pp. 320-25. A detailed discussion on Pareto's views concerning Malthus' population theories is also given by J. J. Spengler, "Pareto in Population I," *Quarterly Journal of Economics,* LVIII (August, 1944), 593-98.

34. Richard Cobden (1804-65), English manufacturer and radical politician who advocated the principles of peace, non-intervention, retrenchment, and free trade throughout his lifetime. The association was formally known as the Anti-Corn Laws League, founded in 1838. I mentioned in the biographical sketch above that while in Florence, Pareto joined the Adam Smith Society founded by Ferrara in opposition to the extension of state powers that occurred in Italy after the fall of the Conservative party (Destra). The *Giornale degli economisti,* founded originally by persons who sided with the State Socialists, was bought up by friends of liberalism and free trade, and Pareto took charge of the monthly political *Cronaca.* For an excellent discussion of Pareto's work on the *Cronaca* see: T. Giacalone-Monaco, "Le 'Cronache' politiche ed economiche di Pareto," *Giornale,* N.S. XIX (Nov.-Dec., 1960), 788-815.

politicians for leading the ignorant astray with their chicanery (Pareto felt there was some truth in this), and also to the refusal of the ignorant to learn. Actually, the advocates of classical doctrines on the Continent, Pareto among them, failed to consider the matter of relevance. The failure of reform leagues, such as the Adam Smith Society, was due to their envisaging what ought to be, paying less attention to what was, starting with very few principles, and assuming the validity of these principles throughout the globe.[35]

Both later defenders of classical political economy (Liberal School), such as Bastiat, and antagonists (the Adversaries), such as Proudhon, made errors similar to those of their predecessors.[36] That is, they exerted themselves to demonstrate that "justice" and "right" are identical with some vaguely defined "utility." Pareto also pointed to the ethical aspects of their works:

Bastiat's work as a whole is devoted to that very thing [justice and right], and that is his purpose especially in his *Economic Harmonies*. Many other writers have also argued the identity of the conclusions of economic science and "morality"—Proudhon, the identity of his economic ideas and "justice." In almost all writers the identity is not between economics and morality as they actually exist in human societies, but between some future economics and some future morality, between economics and morality as they will be at the end—a little known quantity to tell the truth—of an historical evolution. Usually the identity obtained in that manner seems self-evident, for it is assumed implicitly that economics and morality have to be, or are going to be, logical inferences of certain given premises; and it is undeniable that various logical consequences of the same premises cannot be discordant.[37]

The dissenters to the French and English liberal schools developed their own doctrines, which challenged the traditional conclusions of these schools. The German Historical School is one example of these dissenters. There was a tendency among German economists—especially Roscher, Hildebrand, Knies, and Schmoller—to view political economy as an ethical discipline. In fact, according to J. N. Keynes, the school of economics associated with Roscher and Knies called itself ethical and "regarded political economy as having a high ethical task, and as concerning itself with the most important problems of human life."[38]

35. Pareto, *Mind and Society,* III, sec. 2017, pp. 1410-11, admitted to the failure of the Adam Smith Society in Italy.
36. Cf. Gide and Rist, *History,* pp. 290-347.
37. Pareto, *Mind and Society,* IV, sec. 2147 n. 7, p. 1481.
38. John Neville Keynes, *The Scope and Method of Political Economy* (1st ed. 1890; 4th ed. 1917; New York: A. M. Kelly, 1963), pp. 22-23.

Pareto thought that the system of ethics of this school "which was a reaction of nationalistic against cosmopolitan sentiments . . . gave rise to academic socialism, which satisfied the hankering of certain middle-class rationalists who were unwilling to go as far as the cosmopolitan doctrines of Karl Marx."[39] By setting up the "error" of ethics against the "error" of classical economics, the German economists called attention to both. Thus the historical school was no more "experimental" than the classical school, but it laid stress on history, and served to demolish the classical edifice which "soared off into the nebulous realm of metaphysics."[40]

Karl Marx, another dissenter, thought he was getting closer to reality with his theory of surplus value, but he too introduced ethical considerations into his works. That is to say, Marx presented his theory of surplus value in the guise of the capitalists' exploitation of the masses. Pareto did not completely discount the value of Marx's doctrines. Thus, Marx's concept of "class-struggle" was said to have "emphasized the absolute necessity of adding new notions to the concept of economics if one were to arrive at knowledge of concrete realities."[41] Marx helped to tear down the humanitarian edifice of "classical economics based on middle-class interests."[42]

As for two of Pareto's contemporaries, Marshall and Walras, ethical considerations are also found in their works. Marshall gave examples of "practical issues," many of which were ethical in nature, such as: "good" and "evil" of economic freedom, redistribution of income in favor of the "poor," work which is not "elevating in character," the "proper" relations between individual and collective action, the question of how "justifiable" are the methods of distribution of wealth.[43] Yet although he admitted that such issues lay outside the realm of economics for the most part, he went on to say that economics aimed at helping the statesman to determine not only what the end *should* be, "but also what are the best methods of a broad policy devoted to that end."[44]

The scientific basis for these doctrines became stronger as schisms developed. Walras, one of Pareto's contemporaries, was also a reformer breaking with the orthodoxy and yet making definite contributions to economic science in the process. Pareto appreciated the

39. Pareto, *Mind and Society,* III, sec. 2020, p. 1412.
40. *Ibid.*
41. *Ibid.,* sec. 2021, p. 1412.
42. *Ibid.,* sec. 2020, p. 1412.
43. Alfred Marshall, *Principles of Economics* (1st ed. 1890; 8th ed.; London: Macmillan & Co., 1925), p. 41.
44. *Ibid.,* p. 43.

scientific aspects of Walras' works, although he condemned his reform sentiments:

The work of Walras is complex, and becomes intelligible only when we analyse its elements. He himself attached chief importance to it as an expression of a reformer but this is not its leading feature from a scientific point of view. Nevertheless, it was as a movement of reform that what is known as classic political economy took its rise. It was an attempt to break entirely with the past, and to organize society on a fresh basis. It was believed that practical solutions could be obtained through economic science alone.

In the former half of the nineteenth century, this new orthodoxy suffered from a succession of schisms. Some of these were notable as attempts, not always realized as such, to re-establish the balance of ideas disturbed by the one-sided view of 'classic' economics, and to reduce the science of economics to the rank of a branch of social science.

Walras was one of these schismatics, and as such, it may be said of him that he was influenced by his environment. Fortunately, however, for science, he felt the need of laying a solid foundation for his schemes of reformation, and was thus led to re-examine the bases of economics.

In his *Eléments d'économie pure* we read: "Pure political economy is essentially the theory of the determination of values under a hypothetical system of absolutely free competition."

But it is easy to explain Walras' position if we consider the goal at which he aimed. His plan of reform was concerned with a field of economics dominated by free competition; hence he was naturally bent on constructing the theory of that field. Nevertheless, whether he realized it or not, such an inquiry is of service in yet another quest. In analysing what is, in separating by abstraction the different parts of the concrete economic phenomenon, we do find a part that may be termed free competition. Walras has the great merit of having given us the theory of this part considered as a general case.[45]

Although the development of economics as a science was hampered by the inclusion of ethical concepts, sociology had developed even less as a scientific discipline, its doctrines being expounded dogmatically. Pareto also extended his critique of the "unscientific" proclivities of his predecessors and contemporaries to sociology:

Hitherto sociology has nearly always been expounded dogmatically. Let us not be deceived by the word 'positive' that Comte has foisted upon his philosophy. His sociology is as dogmatic as Bossuet's *Discourse on Universal History*. It is a case of two different religions, but

45. Vilfredo Pareto, "Walras," *Economic Journal,* XX (March, 1910), 138-39.

of religions nevertheless; and religions of the same sort are to be seen in the writings of Spencer, DeGreef, LeTourneau, and numberless other authors.

Faith by its very nature is exclusive. If one believes oneself possessed of absolute truth, one cannot admit that there are any other truths in the world. We are by no means asserting that sociologies derived from certain dogmatic principles are useless; just as we in no sense deny utility to the geometries of Lobachevski or Riemann. We simply ask of such sociologies that they use premises and reasonings which are clear and exact as possible. 'Humanitarian' sociologies we have to satiety—they are about the only ones that are being published nowadays. Of metaphysical sociologies (with which are to be classed all positive and humanitarian sociologies) we suffer no dearth. Christian, Catholic, and similar sociologies we have to some extent. Without disparagement to any of those estimable sociologies, we here venture to expound a sociology that is purely experimental after the fashion of chemistry, physics, and other such sciences.[46]

In 1893 Pareto went to Lausanne to cultivate "neutral" and "scientific" economic analysis.[47] The *Cours d'économie politique* was published in 1896.[48] According to Pantaleoni, one of Pareto's closest friends, a large portion of the economic content of the *Cours* was developed by Pareto as a businessman.[49] In the biographical sketch it was noted that during this period he was actively engaged in furthering the cause of *laissez faire*. Therefore it is not surprising that the *Cours* should contain rather strong liberal sentiments, which prompted Wicksell to write:

Throughout his book he [Pareto] reasons as if the gain from exchange were an absolute maximum under free competition, and that it is so for each trading subject. In his treatment of production, distribution, the accumulation of capital, and even in his formulations of monetary theory, this erroneous conception recurs time and again rendering his conclusion invalid. However, he is not as biased as some of the *harmony economists* in their easy optimism that the prevailing distribution of wealth is the manifestly and infallibly sacred outcome of free competition. But as soon as this distribution is accepted as a fact, Pareto says that

46. Pareto, *Mind and Society*, I, sec. 50, p. 26. Again I must caution the reader regarding the term "experimental" as it appears in Livingston's translation. We shall see in Chapter VI that Pareto, who was a physical scientist by training, realized that even *natural* "laws" will not manifest themselves to observation under all conceivable "background conditions," nor can "background conditions" always be controlled in experimentation.
47. T. W. Hutchison, *A Review of Economic Doctrines 1870-1929* (Oxford: Clarendon Press, 1953), p. 217.
48. Vilfredo Pareto, *Cours d'économie Politique* (2 vols.; Lausanne: Librairie de l'Université, 1897). Hereafter referred to as the *Cours*.
49. Pantaleoni, *Economic Journal*, XXXIII, 589.

free competition must provide everyone with the greatest satisfaction of needs (possible in the circumstances) since labour, land and capital are then applied to those uses which give the highest possible yield.[50]

It should be pointed out that Wicksell was not critical of Pareto's sentiments for scientific reasons. It was merely a case of Wicksell's well-known reform sentiments being opposed to the sentiments of Pareto.

Pareto himself was dissatisfied with the *Cours,* as evidenced by his refusal to sanction a reprint[51] and also by his self-criticism in the Preface of the *Manuale di economia politica,* wherein he referred to himself as the "author of the *Cours.*" His main criticism of his earlier work, and perhaps the most devastating he could make from his own point of view, was that he had allowed sentiment to interfere with scientific objectivity. In the following citation we detect the influence of the new developments in scientific thought, which were mainly due to Comtian positivism:

In all the *Cours,* the author considers peace, economic liberty and political liberty, the best means of obtaining the good of the population. But of such propositions he does not give, nor can he give, scientific demonstrations derived only from facts. The belief which is prevalent in the *Cours* transcends, at least for now, objective reality and in great part appears to have its origin in sentiment. Therefore it is absolutely necessary to exclude it from a work which aims at studying facts scientifically.[52]

His great concern for scientific objectivity, evidently related to his own earlier "unscientific" proclivities, caused him to put important emphasis on the subject of scope and method in his later works. Methodological discussions of particular note are contained in *Les Systémes socialistes,* the *Manuale di economia politica,* and the *Trattato di sociologia generale,* as well as in several minor works.[53]

---

50. Knut Wicksell, "Vilfredo Pareto, *Cours d'économie politique,*" *Zeitschrift für Volkswirtschaft, Sozialpolitik und Verwaltung,* (1897), pp. 159-66. Reprinted in English in *Selected Papers of Knut Wicksell,* ed. Erick Lindahl (Cambridge, Mass.: Harvard, 1958), pp. 141-75.

51. Joseph Schumpeter, "Vilfredo Pareto (1848-1923)," *Quarterly Journal of Economics,* LXIII (May, 1949), 157.

52. Pareto, *Manuale,* Preface, p. viii.

53. Cf. Vilfredo Pareto: "Considerazioni sui principii fondamentali dell'economia politica pura," *Giornale degli economisti* (hereafter referred to as *Giornale*), IV (March, 1892), 389-420; (June, 1892), 485-512; V (August, 1892), 119-57; VI (January, 1893), 1-37; VII (October, 1893), 279-321; "Teoria matematica dei cambi forestieri," *Giornale,* VIII (February, 1894), 142-73; "Il modo di figurai i fenomeni economici (A proposito di un libro del dottore Fornasari)," *Giornale,* XII (January, 1896), 75-87; "Sul fenomeno economico. Lettera a Benedetto Croce," *Giornale,* XXI (August, 1900), 139-

Pareto was not unique in his determination to establish an ethically neutral social science. We have seen that both Comte and Marx thought they were stressing "scientific" analysis, yet neither of these writers was able to remain a detached observer. In the end, their systems embodied ethical considerations which reflected their reform sentiments. As for Pareto, he was only partially successful in his endeavor. His economics, as evidenced by his *Manuale,* was surprisingly free of ethical content.[54] His economic theories were not dependent upon any particular system of ethics. For instance, he was able to demonstrate that production unfolds in the same manner (i.e., the coefficients of production may be the same) in an individualistic society, where free competition exists, and in a socialistic society, where the productive services are in the hands of an omnipotent minister of production whose aim it is to attain the maximum collective "ophelimity" (economic utility).[55] Thus we find Pareto rendering a theoretical service to a cause he did not support.[56]

However, the situation with his sociology was quite different. His outlashes against parliamentary democracy, humanitarianism, pacifism, and other popular political and philosophical sentiments of his

---

62; "Sul principio economico," *Giornale,* XXII (February, 1901), 131-38; "Le nuovo teorie economiche. Appunti," *Giornale,* XXIII (September, 1901), 235-52; "Di un nuovo errore nello interpretare le teorie dell'economia matematica," *Giornale,* XXV (Novmeber, 1902), 401-33; "L'interpolazione per la ricerca delle leggi economiche," *Giornale,* XXXIV (March, 1907), 266-85; XXXVI (June, 1908), 423-53; "Economia sperimentale," *Giornale,* LII (July-August, 1918), 1-18; "The New Theories of Economics," *The Journal of Political Economy,* V (September, 1897), 485-502.

54. It might be argued that Pareto's methodological stance—his devotion to "scientific" principles—is also an ethical position, and hence his works are not free of ethical content. This is true, insofar as methodology is a product of philosophical speculation concerned with the problem of the nature and origin of human knowledge. Nevertheless, in this chapter my main concern with Pareto's predecessors and contemporaries lies in their tendency to ignore the subjective minimization of value judgments (this point will emerge as the chapter develops), and not with the philosophical basis of their methodological views. The latter problem will be treated in following chapters.

55. Pareto, *Mind and Society,* II, secs. 1013-1021, 720-722, pp. 405-11, 97-102.

56. Later, Barone, a follower of Pareto, published his famous paper, "Il Ministro della produzione nello stato colletivista," *Giornale,* XXXVII (Sept.-Oct., 1908), 267-93, 391-414, where he further developed the essential arguments of Pareto on the subject. Pareto had anticipated and settled in his own mind a controversy which was to develop thirty years later among Von Mises, Lange, and Knight, on the feasibility of the rational allocation of resources in a socialist economy. Cf. O. Lange and F. M. Taylor, *On the Economic Theory of Socialism* (Minneapolis, Minn.: University of Minnesota Press, 1938), p. 12; Abram Bergson, "Socialist Economics," *Survey of Contemporary Economics,* ed. H. S. Ellis (Homewood, Ill.: Irwin, 1948), pp. 412-48.

time did little to enhance the popularity of his sociology. His sociology can be divided into a scientific part and a political polemic and preceptive part. It is marred, at least as a scientific work, by the latter part. Even Pareto, who preached ethical neutrality and achieved it to a remarkable degree in his economics, could not resist the temptation to depart from his "neutral" position when he turned to sociology.

The question of whether or not Pareto was successful in maintaining an ethical neutrality is not crucial here. What really matters, from the point of view of methodology, is the extent to which he was able to distill the basic issues involved in the problem of ethical neutrality, and how he was able to influence others with his pronouncements. I shall show below that Pareto brought the whole problem of ethical neutrality to the surface in his critique of the unscientific proclivities of his predecessors and contemporaries. His contributions to methodological thought was that he convinced some of his contemporaries, as well as later writers on methodology (especially in England), that a fundamental prerequisite for positive social science was the subjective minimization of ethical judgments ("what ought to be").

PARETO ON THE ETHICAL NEUTRALITY REQUIREMENT

If Pareto was willing to concede that some aspects of ethico-economic doctrines were of service to economic science, and that sociologies derived from dogmatic principles were not useless, why was he critical of them? The answer lies in Pareto's conception of science in general:

Experimental science has no dogmas. . . . And it in truth accepts the proposition that inventions may at times be promoted by non-experimental principles, and does so because that proposition is in accord with results of experience. But so far as demonstration goes, the history of human knowledge clearly shows that all attempts to explain natural phenomena by means of propositions derived from religious or metaphysical principles have failed. Such attempts have finally been abandoned in astronomy, geology, physiology, and all other similar sciences. If traces of them are still to be found in sociology and its sub-branches, law, political economy, ethics, and so on, that is simply because in those fields a strictly scientific status has not yet been achieved.[57]

Hence, by way of analogy with the physical sciences, he believed that the development of political economy and sociology required that the "unscientific" (ethical) principles be abandoned for the principles of the "experimental" sciences. Here we are brought to the very point

57. Pareto, *Mind and Society*, I, sec. 50, p. 26.

that was made in the preceding section regarding non-logico-experimental principles. The use of ethical principles in economics and sociology is not valid from a strictly scientific viewpoint. They are not altered on the basis of experience, and they usually yield moral rather than factual implications. The propositions derived from such principles amount to nothing more than exhortations. The inclusion of ethical principles in economics and sociology would suspend their character as scientific disciplines.

Pareto must share his methodological position regarding positive social science with Weber, who arrived at similar conclusions quite independently. Weber's observations were remarkably similar to Pareto's, at least in substance:

We merely point out that even today the confused opinion that economics does and should derive value-judgements from a specifically "economic point of view" has not disappeared but is especially current, quite understandably, among men of practical affairs.

Our journal [*Archiv für Sozialwissenschaft und Sozialpolitik,* Edgar Jaffé, Werner Sombart, and Max Weber, editors] as the representative of an empirical specialized discipline must reject this view in principle. It must do so because, in our opinion, it can never be the task of empirical science to provide binding norms and ideals from which directives for immediate practical activity can be derived.

An empirical science cannot tell anyone what he *should* do—but rather what he can do. . . . It is true that in our science, personal value-judgements have tended to influence scientific arguments without being explicitly admitted. They have brought about continual confusion. . . .[58]

The above is but one example of several which we shall encounter illustrating the similarity of both authors' methodological views.

We now arrive at a very important juncture in the problem of ethical neutrality. Thus far, Pareto and Weber seem to suggest that a prerequisite for positive social science is the absence of ethical principles. But elsewhere, as I shall show below, they both realized that at best only the subjective minimization of ethical judgments was possible. What is important at this point is that two writers, L. Robbins (whose work made an impressive impact on Anglo-American methodological thought) and T. W. Hutchison, who both claimed Pareto's and Weber's influence upon them, took the former position. They both seemed to argue for the absence of ethical principles. By doing so, they conveyed the incorrect impression that Pareto and Weber

58. Max Weber, *The Methodology of the Social Sciences,* trans. and ed. E. Shils and H. Finch (Glencoe, Ill.: The Free Press, 1949), pp. 52-53.

represented this unqualified point of view. Let us go into the matter in greater detail.

In England, L. Robbins reflected Pareto's and Weber's concern with the ethical nature of economics, with his pronouncement: "But there is nothing in scientific Economics which warrants us in passing these [ethical] judgements. Economics is neutral as between ends. Economics cannot pronounce on the validity of ultimate judgements of value."[59] Robbins was familiar with Pareto, whose works he cited.[60] However, with respect ot his views on "positive" sciences, he seems to have been influenced to a greater degree by Max Weber.[61]

Robbins went so far as to claim that "positive" and "normative" economics were on entirely different planes: "between the generalizations of positive and normative studies there is a logical gulf fixed which no ingenuity can disguise and no juxtaposition in space and time can bridge over."[62] Although he seemed to suggest such a separation, it isn't clear whether Robbins really wanted economic science to be free of welfare considerations.[63]

Another writer who followed Pareto's path in attacking the ethical principles in economic doctrine was T. W. Hutchison.[64] The influence of Pareto upon Hutchison's methodology is quite clear. Hutchison not only repeated Pareto's arguments, but he even adopted terms that were specifically Paretian.[65] He argued that he intended to follow the principles of "scientific" (non-ethical) economics laid down by Pareto, and he added that "Pareto . . . among economists seems to have been one of the first and most emphatic to insist on our principle."[66] However, Hutchison presented Pareto's views in a way that was incorrect in the general impression conveyed. He gave the impression that Pareto was an empiricist in the Comtian sense as discussed in the preceding chapter. Pareto, as we have seen, was critical of Comte's positivism, and certainly was not anti-theoretical.

In his pronouncements on ethical neutrality, Pareto was advocating an ideal. However, he realized that, in practice, some compromise was necessary. He observed that a "man entirely unaffected by

59. Lionel Robbins, *An Essay on the Nature and Significance of Economic Science* (London: Macmillan, 1932), p. 131.
60. *Ibid.*, p. 4, n. 3.
61. *Ibid.*, p. 133.
62. *Ibid.*, p. 132.
63. Cf. M. Blaug, *Economic Theory in Retrospect* (Homewood, Ill.: Irwin, 1962), p. 612.
64. T. W. Hutchison, *The Significance and Basic Postulates of Economic Theory* (London: Macmillan, 1938).
65. Cf. *Ibid.*, pp. 6-16.
66. *Ibid.*, p. 13.

sentiment and free from all bias, all faith, does not exist."[67] Of course, to insist on that complete freedom as a necessary prerequisite to the study of the social sciences would amount to saying that such a study is impossible. Nevertheless, experience has shown that a scientist has a trained capacity for laying aside his sentiments, preconceptions, and beliefs when engaged in scientific pursuit. Pareto himself pointed to Pasteur as an example: "That was the case with Pasteur, who outside his laboratory was a devout Catholic, but inside kept strictly to experimental method. And before Pasteur one might mention Newton, who certainly used one method in discoursing on the Apocalypse and quite another in his *Principia*."[68] He conceded, however, that self-detachment was more readily achieved in the natural sciences than in the social sciences.

Even though complete success in such an effort may not be possible, economists can, conceivably, endeavor to reduce the power and influence of sentiments, preconceptions, and beliefs to a minimum. This is what Pareto was getting at in the following: "It is possible for an author to aim exclusively at hunting out and running down uniformities among facts—their laws, in other words—without having any purpose of direct practical utility in mind, any intuition of offering remedies and precepts, any ambition, even, to promote the happiness and welfare of mankind in general or of any part of mankind. His purpose in such a case is strictly scientific; he wants to learn, to know, and nothing more."[69]

Weber aptly expressed the point Pareto was attempting to make regarding the neutrality requirement for positive social science:

What is really at issue is the intrinsically simple demand that the investigator and teacher should keep unconditionally separate the establishment of empirical facts (including the "value-orientated" conduct of the empirical individual whom he is investigating) and *his* own practical evaluations, i.e., his evaluation of these facts as satisfactory or unsatisfactory (including among these facts evaluations made by empirical persons who are the objects of investigation). These two things are logically different and to deal with them as though they were the same represents a confusion of entirely heterogeneous problems.[70]

In the above, Weber, like Pareto, argues for the *subjective minimization of ethical judgments* in the social sciences.

Some writers in England and Germany denied the possibility of the subjective minimization of ethical judgments, and hence the feasi-

67. Pareto, *Mind and Society*, I, sec. 142, p. 72.
68. *Ibid.*, sec. 142, p. 71.
69. Pareto, *Manuale*, chap. i, sec. 1, p. 3.
70. Weber, *Methodology*, p. 11.

bility of a positive social science. The arguments of some of the Germ-man writers are extremely complex and will be taken up in later chapters. For the present, I shall confine myself to the views of J. A. Hobson, Hawtrey, and Joan Robinson in England. The recent views of Joan Robinson indicate that the issue is still unsettled.

In England some economists would have found Roscher's and Knies's views regarding the ethical nature of economics perfectly acceptable. According to Robbins, J. A. Hobson and Hawtrey believed that economics should not only take account of ethical standards, but should also make pronouncements upon the ultimate validity of these standards.[71] Hawtrey argued that "Economics cannot be disassociated from Ethics."[72] More recently, Joan Robinson has agreed with those who maintained that economics cannot be anything but an ethical discipline.[73] She presents the thesis that all economic doctrine has been an "ideology." From her observations she concludes that there cannot be any such thing as economic "science," having more or less accepted, fatefully, the historical propensity of economists to become involved in ethical problems. Pareto was more optimistic and, as we have seen, felt that the subjective minimization of ethical judgments was possible in the study of human society.

Although today most economists respect Pareto's distinction between "positive" and "normative" economics, this dichotomy has not gone unchallenged; witness, for example, the views of Joan Robinson above. One area where positive and normative economics meet is general economic policy. Here the dichotomy is much more difficult to maintain.

PARETO ON "POSITIVE" POLICY

We have seen that Pareto argued that the subjective minimization of ethical judgments was a fundamental prerequisite for "positive" social science. He also called attention to the need for a "positive" approach to policy in the same way that he advocated "positive" science. Of course, he realized that all policy is normative since it involves questions of "what ought to be." Nevertheless, he made the important distinction between the norms obtaining in the community and the personal ethics of the observer. For Pareto, the subjective minimization of the personal ethics of the observer is absolutely es-

71. For a detailed discussion on the views of Hobson and Hawtrey in this respect, see: Robbins, *Essay,* p. 132.
72. *Ibid.,* p. 133.
73. Joan Robinson, *Economic Philosophy* (Chicago: Aldine, 1962).

sential in matters of policy. In other words, the observer is to take the norms of the community as data, instead of attempting to alter them in keeping with his own subjective views.[74]

The notion of a "correct" policy is meaningful only within the context of the norms obtaining in a community. Consequently, the identification of the "real" norms is absolutely essential before there can be any intelligent discussion of "proper" policy. Therefore it is not surprising that Pareto attempted to develop the apparatus to identify the "real" norms of the community in his sociology.[75] At this point I shall briefly outline some of its implications for policy matters.

According to Pareto, "logico-experimental" reasoning is important where the objectives are known, such as in the arts, crafts, agriculture, industry, commerce, and science. As concerns society itself (the social organism, so to speak), the data of the problems that it must solve are unknown to individuals, and people are moved "more by sentiment than by thought." When an individual in a society believes that society would experience a gain in "utility" by moving in a certain direction, he is only expressing his individual idea of what is best for society. But there are many complex individual utilities in a society, so that to move in a given direction may even result in a social "disutility." In other words, *no one individual or group of individuals acting on the basis of his or their own "subjective" concepts of "utility" possesses the necessary data for "objectively" solving the problem of maximization of social "utility."* This circumstance does not deny the possibility of rational solution (as suggested in the Marxian sociology of knowledge), but suggests that in order to treat the problem, the necessary theoretical apparatus must be developed. Pareto developed the theoretical apparatus in his sociological "utility" theory.[76]

As concerns scientific methodology, Pareto was critical of the writers who implicitly believe that ideologies determine the form of society, that the conduct of human beings is a consequence of their

74. It will be recalled that Pareto's critique of his predecessors was that they often *began* as reformers and used economics to "rationalize" their systems of ethics. In this section, the problem dealt with is slightly different. Assuming the establishment of a "positive" science, the problem of "positive" policy still remains. In other words, once having determined "what is," the economist should not attempt to alter the prevailing situation in keeping with his own subjective norms, but in keeping with the prevailing community norms. This distinction will be elaborated upon in the text.

75. I shall go into Pareto's sociological "utility" theory in the following chapter, in connection with his views on scope. At present my main concern is with the problem of ethical neutrality.

76. Again I must postpone the discussion of Pareto's sociological "utility" theory until the following chapter.

expressed beliefs,[77] and those writers who "rest content with the implicit assumption that observance of the norms of morality always leads to social benefit," never justifying the solution they accept.[78] He was also critical of those who made no distinction between private morality and public affairs.[79]

The distinction between morality and utility is extremely important, for disregard for this distinction has led to many worthless controversies in history. For instance, although the admirers and the critics of the French Revolution are substantially in agreement as to the facts, the former believe that the revolutionists were provoked by the wickedness of their adversaries while the latter see in the revolutionists a disparity of character. Pareto argued that disputes about the French Revolution possess not even the merit of novelty, and that such disputes are replicas of the disputes that have raged, and will forever rage, about every political, social, or religious revolution as long as writers reason "subjectively," applying their own norms, or prevailing norms, in condemning or absolving such actions. Pareto also observed that historical events such as the French Revolution gave rise to ideologies on the part of the contending parties to win support for their cause. The efficacy of these ideologies is not to be judged on their "logical" basis—for by doing so the observer is merely imposing his own norm of rationality on the facts—but on why the "sentiments" and "interests" in question had the success they did. Therefore, the fact that ideologies logically appear "absurd" to the observer is no reason for their being discarded. They may be useful in determining changes in the compositions or intensities of the underlying norms that gave rise to the Revolution or, for that matter, to any other changes in social phenomena.

I turn next to the matter of the policy implications of Pareto's sociology. Solutions to questions of policy will be found in the analysis of the "real" norms, and not in the ideologies which are merely expressions in the form of myths, slogans, ideas, or ideals of the subjective utility concepts of these or those individuals.[80]

77. Pareto, *Mind and Society,* IV, sec. 2060, p. 1433. He pointed to Comte and Spencer in this respect.
78. *Ibid.,* secs. 2161-62, pp. 1502-4.
79. *Ibid.,* sec. 2162, p. 1504. Pareto was suggesting a distinction that is well understood in modern Keynesian economic doctrine: frugality and the avoidance of debt are considered laudable from the individual viewpoint, but in public affairs the pursuit of such a policy may prove harmful rather than beneficial to society.
80. The fact that many ideologies become codified into law does not mean that they are acceptable as norms by which to make judgments of policy. Take for instance the case of "Blue Laws" (which, when enforced, often lead

Pareto was only partially correct. He overlooked the norm-influencing potential of ideologies. Why he did so is a mystery. One likely explanation is that Pareto was interested in answering the following question: How does one go about finding the "real" norms obtaining in a society? The emphasis then is on static equilibrium analysis, and the problem of normative change—a dynamic factor—is separate and distinct.

In spite of the above shortcomings, Pareto did attempt to map out a social goals theory to identify the "real" norms obtaining in society. He realized that a fundamental scientific error occurred when his predecessors introduced personal ethics into matters of policy, instead of identifying the norms of the community. Hence, they were merely advocates rather than impartial observers. In other words, questions of "policy" involve considerations that are only meaningful with reference to the "real" norms obtaining in a society. Historically, this had been the point at which social scientists ceased to be positive scientists and became involved in questions of what ought to be in keeping with their own subjective views. Schumpeter aptly describes the situation:

The fundamental principle that what individuals, groups, and nations actually do must find its explanation in something much deeper than the creeds and slogans that are used in order to verbalize action, conveys a lesson of which modern men—and none more than we economists— stand much in need. We are in the habit when discussing questions of policy of accepting at face value the slogans of our own and, indeed, of a bygone time. We reason exactly as if the Benthamite creed of the eighteenth century had ever been valid. We refuse to realize that policies are politics and to admit to ourselves what politics are.[81]

Pareto's achievement, from a scientific viewpoint, is that he was the first among economists to call attention to the need for a theory of *positive* policy in an area that historically has been normative. Recently, in the proceedings of the American Economic Association, several economists have expressed an interest in the need for a theory of policy. William D. Grampp, for instance, argues:

Although economists have written much about policy, they hardly ever have put their ideas in the form of a reasonably complete theory; i.e., a statement of the values that direct policy, their origin and order

---

to public hostility towards the enforcement officers), or the case of the popularity of "bootlegging" in "dry" states. All such cases are examples of the heterogeneous nature of individual utilities.

81. Schumpeter, *Quarterly Journal of Economics*, LXIII, 173.

of importance, the economic means of realizing them, and a defense of why the values and means are appropriate.

. . . .

As everyone knows, a debate over policy can be improved by someone interjecting, "Let's get the theory straight!" Why not get the history straight, too?

In getting it straight we would uncover some curious information about the temperament economists have displayed toward policy. They have not had as much interest in it as in positive economics, and the interest they have had has been about particular problems more than about systems or theory.

. . . .

Knowing this helps us to understand the attitude of others towards us. "To hell with economics—let's build a better world," it was said recently. I am disgusted with such ignorance and alarmed. But I am not surprised. We have not made it altogether clear to the world what we think about its prospects, and what we have said has not always been accurate. That is shown by the place of economics in the history of policy.[82]

Although Pareto's methodological contribution to the theory of positive policy has generally been overlooked by the economics profession, it is particularly relevant in the light of the above observations.

In summary, until Pareto's time, economic doctrine was very often the expression of economic, political, or social reformers who attempted to "rationalize" one favored system of ethics or another. The tendency to regard economics as an ethical discipline, either implicitly or explicitly, continued with Pareto's contemporaries. This is not to say, of course, that many of Pareto's contemporaries did not distinguish between "positive" and "ethical" problems. I simply point out that in their own works they failed to minimize ethical considerations.

One implication of the propensity of economists to include ethical considerations in their works was that many of the polemics that occurred in economics involved disputes over what ought to be rather than what is. Ethical disputes contributed to the development of economic science only in a negative way. That is to say, while the participants in the polemics called attention to the ethical aspects of the economic doctrines of their adversaries, they, in turn, advocated their own favored system of ethics.[83]

82. William D. Grampp, "On the History of Thought and Policy," *American Economic Review*, LX (May, 1965), 128-42.

83. It is one thing to make an assumption for theoretical purposes; it is quite another thing to accept a theoretical assumption as a normative principle. For example, Walras did not look upon his assumption of "free" competition

Pareto's attack on the ethical aspects of the doctrines of his predecessors and contemporaries, as well as his views on the neutrality requirement, represented a definite contribution to the development of economic science. He brought the whole problem of ethical neutrality to the surface with his pronouncements. By doing so he was able to convince some of his contemporaries, as well as later writers on methodology, that a fundamental requirement for positive science was the subjective minimization of ethical judgments. Two outstanding writers, L. Robbins and T. W. Hutchison, whose works on methodology made an impressive impact on Anglo-American methodological thought, were directly influenced by him. However, both writers take a more "positivistic" stance than Pareto, by suggesting the elimination of ethical principles as a necessary condition for "positive" science.

Today most economists respect the distinction between "positive" and "normative" economics. Recall though, that the issue of ethical neutrality was far less clear in Pareto's time. It is to Pareto's great merit that he was among the first of economists (together with Weber) to expound the principles of positive ("logico-experimental") social science.[84]

Pareto's achievement does not end with the above. He was the first among economists to call attention to the need for a theory of "positive" policy, in an area that historically has been normative. Although Pareto's methodological contribution to the theory of "positive" policy has been overlooked, it is particularly relevant in the light of recent discussions on the problem.

---

merely as a theoretical assumption. On the basis of this assumption he concluded that "free" competition would result in the greatest "utility" for the individuals in a society. He then went on to advocate free competition and accepted it as a normative principle. The same situation occurred with the classical assumption of free trade.

84. I might point to the practical significance of positive social science with the example of Soviet economics. Here is a case, outside the Pareto and Weber sphere of influence, where ideology has long dominated and suffocated the development of rational economic analysis. Only recent changes have shown promise.

IV The Scope of Economics and Sociology

INTRODUCTION

In the introductory chapter (pp. 25-26) I mentioned that both Comte and the German economists attacked classical economics as speculative and unrealistic, although their reasons for doing so differed. As far as I am able to determine, the critique of classical economics was based on two distinct methodological issues, which were never clearly distilled by the participants in the polemic. One issue, relevant to the problem of scope, was whether specialized disciplines were valid in the social sciences. Comte and many of the German writers denied the validity of specialized analytical disciplines in the social sciences for reasons which will be considered in this chapter.[1] Another methodological issue involved in the polemic was the distinction between the methodologies of the physical and social sciences. In the following chapter I shall examine the problem of the validity of theoretical generalizations in the social sciences.

If the arguments of Comte and the German writers were accepted, the problem of delimiting the scope of any specialized discipline would not exist, since there could only be one unified social science. If their views on scope were denied, then the question would arise: precisely what is the subject of study for each of the specialized disciplines? In other words, one would be presented with the problem of delimiting the boundaries of the individual social sciences. These two problems—specialized disciplines versus the conception of

---

1. Comte and most of the German economists were reformers. Historically, reformers have had a tendency to prefer broad scope, i.e., political, ethical, etc., as well as economic. In this chapter the main concern is with the *methodological* basis for writers' views on scope.

one unified social science, and the delimitation of the scope of economics—will be the main interest of this chapter.

Although specialized analytical disciplines contributed greatly to knowledge by investigating particular aspects of concrete human actions in depth, they also contributed to the fragmentation of knowledge. The problem of fragmentation and its methodological implications will also be discussed in this chapter.

The views of Marshall and Weber will be presented in juxtaposition to those of Pareto. I have several reasons for my choice of Marshall and Weber. For one, they were contemporaries of Pareto, so that in considering their views I am able to present the contemporary issues in their historical context. Also, Marshall and Weber were perhaps the leading professional figures in their respective countries—England and Germany—during the period. Hence their opinions are of great import. Finally, both writers, in turn, were influenced to some extent by the intellectual traditions characteristic of their countries—English utilitarianism and classical economics, and German idealistic social thought and the German historical school. Both Marshall and Weber were products of the intellectual traditions of their respective countries although both writers' works represented departures, in certain respects, from the older traditions. Pareto was a follower of the third intellectual tradition discussed in the introductory chapter—Comtian positivism. His views, too, represented a departure from the older intellectual tradition that had influenced him. We have already seen, at least in certain respects, how Pareto's views on the "scientific approach" represented a departure from those of Comte. So in contrasting Pareto's views with those of Marshall and Weber, I will be contrasting the modifications in thought that took place in these intellectual traditions during the period in which Pareto lived. I shall contrast Pareto's views mainly with those of Marshall and Weber although other writers will also be considered.

In certain respects the topics of scope and method are interrelated, which presents a problem of organization. In so far as I am able, I shall confine the discussion of methodology in this chapter to those areas that have a direct bearing on the problem of scope, and leave the issue of method for discussion in the following chapter.

THE PROBLEM OF SCOPE IN ITS HISTORICAL CONTEXT

Economics had its pre-history, and suggestions of what later became a specialized discipline are found in the writings of the Greeks and Romans, the Scholastics, the Natural Law philosophers, and the mercantilists.[2] However, economic discussions were subordinated, in most cases, to intellectual, moral, ethical, and political analysis. It is difficult to establish precisely at what point in its development economics became a separate intellectual discipline. The works of Petty, North, Locke, Cantillon, and Hume represented a transitional phase in the development of economics as a specialized discipline. Nevertheless, economics did not emerge as a separate discipline until the advent of the writings of Quesnay and Adam Smith.[3] The physiocrats at first called themselves "Economists," using the word as a proper noun.[4] When this designation ceased to be distinctive they used the name "physiocrats," which in turn was abandoned. The influence of physiocratic doctrine upon the works of Adam Smith is well known.[5] What is important here is that Smith's total works represented a specialized division of concrete human activities. In his *Theory of Moral Sentiments* the subject of his interest was *homo ethicus,* while in the *Wealth of Nations* he dealt with *homo oeconomicus.*[6] Hence the activities of the abstract man, *homo oeconomicus,* in his pursuit of wealth, were systematically analysed by Smith in his later researches.

Ricardo followed Smith's path with the tacit assumption that no motive of action except the desire for wealth needed to be considered by the economist.[7] Later, J. S. Mill defined political economy as a science dealing with the combined operations of mankind for the production and distribution of wealth.[8] Bagehot, in his *Economic Studies,* expressed a definition similar to that of Mill, while adding that political economy "deals not with the entire real man as we

2. Cf. Eric Roll, *A History of Economic Thought* (Englewood Cliffs, N.J.: Prentice-Hall, 1939), pp. 19-87; Joseph Schumpeter, *History of Economic Analysis* (New York: Oxford University Press, 1954), pp. 51-378 for the individual writers of the period.
3. François Quesnay, *Tableau économique* (Paris: Institut national d'études démographiques, 1958). See n. 6, below, for Smith's major works.
4. Edward Heimann, *History of Economic Doctrines* (New York: Oxford, 1964), p. 52.
5. For a discussion of the influence of the physiocrats, as well as that of Francis Hutchison, upon Adam Smith see Edwin Cannan's "Editor's Introduction" in *The Wealth of Nations* (New York: Modern Library, 1937), pp. xxiii-lvi.
6. Adam Smith, *The Theory of Moral Sentiments* (2 vols.; "last English edition"; Boston: Wells and Lilly, 1827); *An Inquiry into the Nature and Causes of the Wealth of Nations* (London: A. Strahan and T. Cadell, 1793).
7. J. N. Keynes, *The Scope and Method of Political Economy* (4th ed. 1917; New York: A. M. Kelley, 1963), p. 116.
8. J. S. Mill, *Essays on Some Unsettled Questions of Political Economy* (London: J. W. Parker, 1844), p. 125.

know him . . . but with a simpler, imaginary man. . . ."[9] In other words, the economist was to take as the subject of his study the actions of an abstract economic man rather than the actions of concrete man. Thus the scope of economics was delimited according to areas of action as well as method. Of course, this is not to say that these writers actually confined their discussions to purely economic man, but that they tended to stress the economic aspects of human actions in their analyses.

The tendency to define the scope of economics according to the area of action continued in the works of Marshall and Pareto, with some refinements. These refinements will be discussed in greater detail below.

Pareto considered discussions regarding the classification of various specialized disciplines a waste of time, because "the division of knowledge into parts is artificial and certainly not rigid, changing with time to meet the purposes of particular researches."[10] Marshall took a similar view by arguing that it would be better if we troubled ourselves less "with scholastic inquiries as to whether a certain consideration comes within the scope of economics."[11] Both, however, held definite views on scope, and they were not reluctant to discuss them.

Pareto was not willing to place strict limitations on the scope of economics. Yet, some indications of limits implicitly emerge from his works. To begin, he gave as the scope of his study in the *Cours* the following: "The objects of our study are the phenomena which result from the actions which men accomplish for procuring the things which bring satisfaction to their needs and desires. Hence it is necessary to examine the nature of the relations which intercede between the things and the satisfaction of these needs and desires and to try then to discover the laws of the phenomena which have precisely such relations as principle cause."[12] For Pareto then, economics had as its scope the study of those phenomena that resulted from man's attempt to satisfy his material wants.

Marshall was less clear on this point. On the one hand he stated that economists dealt with man "as he is," that is, not with an "abstract or 'economic man'" but with a "flesh and blood man."[13] He

9. W. Bagehot, *Economic Studies* (London: Longmans, 1888), p. 5.

10. Vilfredo Pareto, *The Mind and Society,* trans. and ed. A. Livingston (4 vols.; New York: Harcourt, Brace and Co., 1935), I, sec. 2, p. 3.

11. Alfred Marshall, *Principles of Economics* (1st ed. 1890; 8th ed.; London: Macmillan & Co., 1925), p. 27.

12. Vilfredo Pareto, *Cours d'économie politique* (2 vols.; Lausanne: Librairie de l'Université, 1897), I, sec. 3, p. 10.

13. Marshall, *Principles,* p. 27.

seemed to be suggesting that economics dealt with man's total concrete behavior rather than with only certain aspects of his behavior.
But then he went on to say that although economists dealt with man
as "he is," they were concerned chiefly with "man's conduct in the
business part of his life."[14] However, by dealing with the "business
part" of man's life, Marshall concentrated his attention on one aspect
of man's concrete behavior; and in substance he came very close to
Pareto's view. Elsewhere, the closeness of views of the two writers is
revealed in Marshall's statement that "economics deals with man's
efforts to satisfy his wants."[15]

In addition, both authors thought that economic phenomena had
the advantage of lending themselves to precise quantitative measurements. For Marshall, the "force" of a person's motives could be
approximately measured in terms of money.[16] He went so far as to say
that: "The *raison d'être* of economics as a separate science is that it
deals chiefly with that part of man's action which is most under con-
trol of measurable motives; and which therefore lends itself better
than any other to systematic reasoning and analysis.[17] Since Marshall
believed that economics dealt with man's efforts to satisfy his wants
only "in so far as efforts and wants are capable of measurement," he
made an additional qualification as to the scope of economics. This
quantitative qualification differed sharply from the views of the German and Austrian writers, who were also concerned with the qualitative aspects of economic phenomena.[18] Pigou, a follower of Marshall, gave greater clarity to Marshall's qualification by saying that
"though no precise boundary between economic and non-economic
welfare exists, yet the test of accessibility to a money measure serves
well enough to set up a rough distinction."[19] Pareto saw economic
phenomena as lending themselves not only to quantitative measurements, but also to the logic of mathematics as exemplified by Walras,
Edgeworth, Fisher, and other "mathematical" economists.

In summarizing, I would not do violence to Pareto's and Marshall's views if I attributed as common to them the following definition: economics has as its scope the study of phenomena that result
from man's attempt to satisfy his material wants, in so far as such

14. *Ibid.*, p. 14.
15. *Ibid.*, p. 49.
16. *Ibid.*, p. 15.
17. *Ibid.*, p. 39.
18. *Ibid.*, p. 49. Menger, we recall, objected to mathematics because it
prevented economists from getting to the qualitative "essence" of value, rent,
and profit.
19. Arthur Pigou, *The Economics of Welfare* (London: Macmillan, 1920),
p. 11.

phenomena are quantitative and hence capable of mesurement. Admittedly, the definition is rather general, and the precise boundary location is somewhat unclear. Both authors were unwilling to commit themselves to greater limitations. Even so, they were unable to confine their studies to these generalities. It might be worthwhile to mention each writer's conception of economic "science." We saw earlier that Pareto viewed economics as a "positive" science, concerned with *what is*. Marshall took a similar position. Arguing that economics is a "science pure and applied, rather than a science and an art,"[20] he cautioned the economist to shun many "political" issues that a "practical" man cannot ignore.

What is important for the purposes of this chapter is that all the writers mentioned above were representative of a point of view that accepted as valid the delimitation of the scope of economics according to a specific class of human actions. This view was severely challenged by Comte as well as the German writers. For Comte, the extremely intimate connection between the phenomena of wealth and other aspects of social life precluded any attempt to separate economic science from a more general social science. Social reality could best be approximated through a science of society—sociology.

The Germans' critique of the tendency to limit economics according to a specific area of action was very similar to that of Comte, although they differed with him on methods. Comte found the analytical methods of the physical sciences perfectly acceptable, while for the Germans, history was the indispensable tool for the study of human society.

Although Pareto supported the English economists in his defense of specialized disciplines, he was also sympathetic towards the views of Comte and the German economists regarding the problem of the fragmentation of knowledge. I shall show below that Pareto's contribution to the issue of scope lay in his attempt to reconcile the opposing views of the English and the Continental economists. The remainder of this chapter will be devoted to the basis of his defense of specialized disciplines on the one hand, and his attempt to overcome the problem of fragmentation on the other hand.

THE NECESSITY FOR SPECIALIZED DISCIPLINES IN THE STUDY
OF HUMAN SOCIETY

In Chapter II we saw that one of the essential points of view that resulted from detailed historical research in Germany, and

20. Marshall, *Principles,* p. 41.

which the historical school helped to establish generally, was "the unity of social life" and the inseparable connection between its elements.[21] We saw also that, essentially, the advocates of this view argued that social phenomena were capable of interpretation only in all their historical facets—economic, ethical, legal, cultural, etc. This meant that "social reality" did not permit the "isolation" of particular facts, that the concrete facts offered by historical research could not be "dissected" without loss. Another point of view closely associated with that of the "unity of social life," at least for the problem of scope, was "organicism." One meaning of the term was that the whole was something greater than the sum of its parts. Here again the claim was that "social reality" did not permit a breaking down of the total social organism into its parts. As concerns the problem of scope, both the "unity of social life" and "organistic" views led to the viewing of society in terms of a social *whole*. For simplicity I shall refer to all such views, in their relation to scope, as the "unity of social life" views.[22] The "unity of social life" views involved a desire to replace the alleged "unrealistic" specialized studies with a comprehensive view of the whole of reality.[23] From a scientific viewpoint, this desire presented implications regarding the definitional problem of scope, for it denied validity to the boundaries of economics according to a specialized area of actions and suggested the idea of a universal social science. Hence, this point of view cannot be ignored in a dis-

---

21. When Schumpeter speaks of the "historical school" he has in mind that associated with the name of Schmoller. "First a 'school' which became a force in our science and which could call forth or influence analogous movements in other countries developed only under Schmoller's leadership" (*Economic Doctrine and Method,* trans. R. Aris (London: George Allen and Unwin, 1954), p. 156). For those who feel that this designation would be a disparagement of the contributions of Roscher, Hildebrand, and Knies, Schumpeter is willing to designate these writers as the "older" school. Later, in his *History of Economic Analysis,* Schumpeter revises his classifications and gives the following designation: "The 'Older' Historical School": Hildebrand, Roscher, Knies; "The 'Younger' Historical School": Schmoller and Brentano, Bucher, Held, Knapp; "The 'Youngest' Historical School": Spiethoff, Sombart, Max Weber (pp. 808-20). My references to the German historical school will be specifically to those represented by Schmoller's influence, in keeping with Schumpeter's earlier designation, unless otherwise indicated. As concerns Spiethoff, Sombart, and Weber, although they were influenced by Schmoller in their formative years, they felt a greater tolerance for deductive theorizing than did their predecessor. This will emerge from my presentation of Max Weber's views.

22. The dynamic aspects of the organistic viewpoint—where society is seen as an evolving thing, analogous to biological organisms—will not be discussed in this chapter. To introduce the problem of statics and dynamics would only complicate an already difficult discussion.

23. Cf. Schumpeter, *Economic Doctrine,* p. 176.

cussion of scope. Both Pareto and Weber were critical of this view, for similar reasons, and their arguments will be presented together.[24]

One argument of the advocates of the "unity of social life" views was that historical reality was too complex to be grasped by the abstractions that form the basis for specialized study, such as "economic man," "political man," etc. Specialized disciplines, it was argued, were only valid for the study of physical phenomena, which could be analyzed separately. Weber agreed that "concrete historical reality" is so complex and diverse as not to be completely grasped by such concepts. But he argued that the complexity of reality in itself is not a reason for the common differences between the physical and social sciences. Specialized studies of "nature" do not formulate total concrete reality, but only certain aspects represented by abstraction. For example, chemistry and physics do not deal with *total* concrete reality. The same situation applies to the study of human society; so that from a logical point of view the physical and social sciences are in the same position—neither can furnish complete representations of total, concrete reality, and both must confine themselves to the scientific purposes at hand.

Regarding the necessity and nature of abstractions as a basis for specialized disciplines, both Pareto and Weber realized that no logical distinction existed between the physical and social sciences.[25] One of the tasks of scientific training is to enable individuals to distinguish the parts in a concrete whole by an analytical process. This process, known as abstraction, is characteristic of all sciences. The necessity for such abstraction results from two circumstances: the limitation of human capabilities, and the subtlety, complexity, and elusiveness of phenomena which occur in the concrete environment. Hence, in order to achieve any worthwhile measure of understanding, it becomes nec-

24. The most accurate and elaborate studies of Max Weber's methodology are: Alexander von Schelting, *Max Weber's Wissenschaftslehre* (Tübingen: Mohr, 1934); Talcott Parsons, *The Structure of Social Action* (York, Pa.: McGraw-Hill, 1937), pp. 500-694; Reinhard Bendix, *Max Weber: An Intellectual Portrait* (Garden City, N. Y.: Doubleday, 1960). Perhaps Weber's most complete statement on the subject is in *Wirtschaft und Gesellschaft,* originally printed as the third part of *Grundriss der Sozialökonomik* (2 vols.; Tübingen: Mohr, 1914), and reprinted in *Gesammelte Aufsätze zur Wissenschaftslehre* (Tübingen: Mohr, 1922), hereafter referred to as *Wissenschaftslehre.* Certain of his essays on methodology were translated and published by Edward A. Shils and Henry A. Finch, *Max Weber on the Methodology of the Social Sciences* (Glencoe, Ill.: The Free Press, 1949), hereafter referred to as *Methodology.*

25. Pareto, *Mind and Society,* I, sec. 25, p. 17. Weber, *Wissenschaftslehre,* pp. 65-67. This argument also emerges in Weber's critique of Eduard Meyer's methodological views (see: *Methodology,* pp. 114-15).

essary to separate the concrete whole into parts, or, to paraphrase Pareto: political economy studies the abstract man *"homo oeconomicus,"* who discharges certain economic actions; *"homo ethicus"* is considered for moral study, *"homo religiosus"* is the subject of religious study, etc.[26] These "individuals" are abstractions in so far as "concrete human action" involves some combination of them.

Another argument in support of the "unity of social life" view placed importance on the philosophy of history, and emphasized the total cultural *Gestalten* of wholes in their unique individuality as opposed to traditional economic theory. In answer, both Pareto and Weber pointed out that this argument reflected an erroneous impression of what constitutes a cultural totality. That is to say, the "whole" that is chosen by the observer is never a simple reproduction of immediately given experience, but involves selection and systematization of the elements of this experience. This selection and systematization involves relating experience to concepts which serve as a basis for giving the significance of the elements of experience to the whole. To use Weber's words:

> Even the first step towards an historical judgement is thus—this is to be emphasized—a process of *abstraction*. This process proceeds through the analysis and mutual isolation of the components of the directly given data—which are to be taken as a complex of possible causal relations—and should culminate in a synthesis of the "real" causal complex. Even this first step thus transforms the given "reality" into an historical fact. In Goethe's words, "theory is involved in the 'fact'."[27]

Among these "mental constructs" are those concepts which form the basis for specialized disciplines, such as *homo oeconomicus*.

Pareto took a position similar to Weber's. He maintained that we can never know all aspects of the concrete whole; and moreover, even if we were capable of having a "complete view" of this whole, it would be prolix to include facts that bore little relevance to the purpose of the study.[28] Also, Pareto argued that the concept of the "reality of the whole" involved a contradiction, since, by choosing certain facts occurring in a given time and neglecting others, it is necessary to abstract to a certain degree from concrete reality.[29]

26. Vilfredo Pareto, *Manuale d'economia politica* (Milano: Società editrice libraria, 1906), chap. i, sec. 15, p. 11.
27. Weber, *Methodology,* p. 173.
28. Pareto, *Mind and Society,* I, secs. 39, 106, pp. 22, 25.
29. Pareto, *Manuale,* chap. i, sec. 5, pp. 5-6.

The arguments in support of the "unity of social life" view may be interpreted as opposing an organic social realm to a mechanistic nature whose parts are not internally related to each other. The argument would then be that the social organism cannot be analyzed in a mechanistic manner without distortion. Here I need only point to a *biological* science analogy. Although it would be absurd to deny the interdependency of the biological processes in the human organism, such an interdependency does not preclude specialized medical research. The efficacy of specialized medical research is beyond question. Another point is also worth mention. Even if the human organism is viewed as a whole (internally related parts), there is no reason why this view should approximate immediate perception. For instance, the human organism can be studied as a *system* of interdependent chemical processes, hence abstracting from its physical structure. Pareto applied the same reasoning to his study of human society. He did not look upon society as an entity whose "reality" was found in its description. On the contrary, he spoke of a social *system* through which he tried to grasp the totality of the *forces* at work. This system was an abstraction, rather than a concrete entity, which accounted for the interdependency of social phenomena. I shall discuss Pareto's system in greater detail below in conjunction with his theory of policy.

Although Pareto and Weber were unfamiliar with each other's works, both were critical—for similar reasons—of the German historical school's arguments of the "unity of social life" as a reason for denying the validity of specialized disciplines in the social sciences. The similarity of Pareto's and Weber's views is important to the history of scientific methodology. As later members of two entirely different intellectual traditions—Pareto, positivism; Weber, German idealism—the similarities of their views represent a convergence of thought and a logical reconciliation of the earlier differences that existed between these intellectual traditions. I say "logical" because both authors were influenced by their respective intellectual traditions, so that their actual methods are quite distinct. This latter point will be discussed in greater detail in the following chapter.

The definitional problem of scope would be radically different depending on which methodological view is taken—the historical school, or that represented by Pareto and Weber.[30] Schumpeter re-

---

30. In practice Weber was never able to remove himself completely from the influence of German social thought, and his works, like those of Marx, were a kind of "economic sociology." These distinctions will become clearer as the chapter develops.

flects on this aspect of the views of the historical school and aptly expresses the point that Pareto and Weber were also expressing:

> There was even a tendency to venture into regions without any bounds. The further the development of the individual discipline in the field of social sciences progresses, the more nebulous and remote becomes the idea of universal social science and the more imperfect any summary is bound to become. To abandon the specialized discipline of economics almost means the abandonment of the possibility of progress itself, since the economist would be alienated from his task. And yet this abandonment was almost complete in Germany.[31]

For Pareto, as well as the English economists, scope had to do with the delimitation of the subject matter of the specialized disciplines which together constituted the social sciences. This is the more common view today.[32] Recall, though, that Pareto wrote in a period when this view was severely challenged by the historical school.

THE INTERDEPENDENCY OF SOCIAL PHENOMENA[33]

Although the above arguments in support of the "unity of social life" view were somewhat tenuous, there was a great deal of substance in the German economists' concern for the fragmentation of knowledge that occurred with specialized disciplines. It is true that specialized analytical disciplines contribute greatly to knowledge by investigating areas of concrete human action in depth. However, since these disciplines deal only with *aspects* of the concrete whole, concrete phenomena will always contain properties outside the scope of a particular specialized science.

In the case of economics, when economists turn to practical problems—general economic policy, for instance—they are confronted

31. Schumpeter, *Economic Doctrine*, p. 176 n. 1. An important consequence of this abandonment was the weak development of economic theory in Germany.

32. Paul A. Samuelson, *Economics: An Introductory Analysis* (1st ed. 1948; 6th ed.; New York: McGraw-Hill, 1956), p. 5, tells us that economists today generally agree on a definition like the following: "Economics is the study of how men and society *choose,* with or without the use of money, to employ *scarce* productive resources to produce various commodities over time and distribute them for consumption, now and in the future, among various people and groups in society." Although he emphasizes choice and scarcity, the subject matter of economics is delimited according to a specific area of action.

33. My main concern in this section is with the "interdependency of *social* phenomena" concept, and its implications for individual specialized disciplines which together constitute the social sciences. The interdependency of *economic* phenomena, and the models developed to take account of such interdependency, will be discussed in Chapter VI.

with non-economic problems as well. The interdependency of economic and other social phenomena is such that very often attempts to deal with policy issues from strictly economic considerations have been far from impressive.[34] I have already mentioned the failure of the Adam Smith Society and other Continental *laissez faire* advocates in this connection. They ignored the matter of the *relevance* of the economic doctrines that they expounded. When the question of relevance is introduced to economic theory, social institutions come to the foreground. Schmoller was correct in his assessment that the principles embodied in the system of classical economics were not universal, but rather an expression of a *Geist* characterized by liberalism, individualism, commercialism, and *Manchestertum*. The practical usefulness of the classical system was limited to the social circumstances identified by these characteristics only.[35]

Pareto reached conclusions similar to those of Schmoller, at least in substance. Significantly, contrary to Schmoller, he was a staunch supporter of specialized researches by area of action. Yet, he realized that specialized disciplines had their limitations when applied to concrete problems. Pareto, the economist, tells us in his own words on the occasion of his jubilee at the University of Lausanne, July, 1917:

Having arrived at a certain point in my researches in political economy, I found myself in a way without outcome. I saw the experimental truth and could not explain it. [Take for example, the case of "free trade" and high protective tariffs coexisting among different countries seemingly having no effect on their prosperity.] Many obstacles presented themselves to me: among others, the interdependency of social phenomena, which did not entirely permit the isolating of studies of these different types of phenomena and which are opposed to the progress of one of them indefinitely if it is deprived of the help of others. It is without doubt that very often the conclusions of economic theory are not verified by experience, and we find ourselves embarrassed to make them correspond. How to overcome this difficulty?[36]

Pareto set out to overcome this difficulty by *supplementing* economic theory with sociological theory, in order to render a better approximation to concrete reality. The above citation is very important because

34. To go into the history of policy would be beyond the scope of this study. For a brief, but well-documented, history of policy and its shortcomings, see: William D. Grampp, "On the History of Thought and Policy," *American Economic Review*, LV (May, 1965), 128-42.

35. However, the *Geist* also included a "scientific spirit," so that Schmoller was somewhat biased in his assessment.

36. Gino Borgatta, "I rapporti fra la scienza economica e la sociologia nell'opera Paretiana," *Giornale degli economisti*, LXIV (Jan.-Feb., 1924), p. 85, n. 1.

it reveals the nature of Pareto's interest in sociology. Pareto, the economist, was interested in the practical implications of economic theory. Schumpeter is one of the few economists to fully appreciate Pareto's special interest in sociology: "It is, therefore, quite understandable that he [Pareto] should have experienced a wish and, in fact, a need to erect, alongside his pure theory another building that would shelter facts and reasonings of a different kind, facts and reasonings that would do something toward answering the question how the element taken care of by his economic theory might be expected to work out in practical life."[37] The practical implication of economic theory with which Pareto was really concerned was general policy. He realized that general policy is intimately bound up in politics; therefore it is not surprising that his sociology was a sociology of the political process.[38]

Of course, Pareto was not alone in his recognition of the intimate relationship between economic and other social phenomena.[39] I have already mentioned the views of the German economists and Comte in this connection. In addition to Pareto, such economic sociologists as Marx and Weber attempted systematic studies that explicitly analyzed the relationship between economic and other social (non-economic) phenomena.[40] At the far end of the spectrum were Comte and Spencer, who were avowedly sociologists. For them, there was no legitimate distinction between economic and non-economic phenomena; instead they treated all human phenomena as part of a general science of society.

37. Joseph Schumpeter, "Vilfredo Pareto (1848-1923)," *Quarterly Journal of Economics,* LXIII (May, 1949), 167.

38. I have already discussed the political orientation of Pareto's sociology in the introductory chapter. Schumpeter sensed Pareto's limited interest in sociology, i.e., that his was a sociology of the political process. The Italian economists, in general, understood Pareto's special interest in sociology.

39. The significance of his contribution lies in his method. This aspect will be discussed in the following section.

40. With respect to the theory of the public household, Wicksell's main contribution was his position that budget determination is a political and not a market process. See: Knut Wicksell, *Finanztheoretische Untersuchungen* (Jena: 1896); excerpts translated into English and reprinted as: "A New Principle of Just Taxation," *Classics in the Theory of Public Finance,* Richard A. Musgrave and Alan T. Peacock, eds. (New York: Macmillan, 1962), pp. 72-118. Erik Lindahl, following Wicksell's lead, also recognized the "sociopolitical" aspects in connection with a "just" distribution of income. See: Erik Lindahl, *Die Gerechtigkeit der Besteuerung* (Lund: Gleerupska, 1919); excerpts translated into English and reprinted as: "Some Controversial Questions in the Theory of Taxation," *Classics in the Theory of Public Finance,* pp. 214-32. However, the scope of their interest in the relationship between economic and non-economic phenomena was less general than that of the writers mentioned in the text.

In the case of Marshall, although on a theoretical level his work appeared to be strictly economic, his complete system contained non-economic elements which made it a kind of an applied sociology. For Marshall, money became the quantifying factor in the supply-and-demand relationships characteristic of his work. But if he were to confine himself to discussing human actions in their functional relation to price, his analysis would exclude many non-economic (using his definition of economics) variables that are also important factors in supply and demand. He did refuse, however, to confine his interests to price-quantity relationships, and actually expanded the scope of his works to include non-economic factors.

I need only consider Marshall's demand analysis in order to support my position that he included non-economic elements in his "economics." In connection with demand, Marshall discussed three types of wants. Two of these were treated as given—biological needs, and artificial wants such as "the wanton vagaries of fashion." The third was a particular type of want associated with human development: "each step upwards is to be regarded as the development of new activities giving rise to new wants."[41] For Marshall, wants adjusted to "activities" form a "standard of life" and offer a satisfaction which "affords strength" to labor. These are activities which are pursued as ends and which form the noblest qualities of human character. They contribute to the development of the character of human life by an "increase of intelligence and energy and self-respect; leading to more care and judgment in expenditures, and to an avoidance of food and drink that gratify the appetite but afford no strength and of ways of living that are unwholesome physically and morally."[42] In the way of a concrete description of these activities, he had in mind: rationality, frugality, industry, honorable dealings, energy, initiative, and enterprise. These wants, together with the "activities" upon which they depended, did not strictly fit into economics (using Marshall's definition) since they were merely *descriptions* of a broader cultural totality, more properly sociological. Marshall was describing a *Geist*, in the German sense, a unifying concept which tied together economic, ethical, political, etc. characteristics of a particular society. Furthermore, such characteristics were not even "forces" which "can be approximately measured in terms of money," i.e., price-quantity relationships. Yet they were not treated as given, as in the case of the two other wants mentioned. On the contrary, they were an important

41. Marshall, *Principles*, p. 89. The above discussion on Marshall's "wants and activities" relies on Parsons, *Structure*, chap. iv.
42. Marshall, *Principles*, p. 689.

factor in Marshall's demand (and also supply) theory. Marshall, recognizing the limitations of confining his study to human actions in their functional relation to price, included "activities" in his works. This inclusion served as a counterweight to "utility economics" and broadened its scope considerably. As Parsons has pointed out, Marshall's economics was applied sociology.[43]

One possible reason for Marshall's propensity to include non-economic elements in his "economics" was his pronounced empiricist leaning, which made him deeply distrustful of "long chains of deductive reasonings."[44] With regards to abstracting from the concrete environment, he had this to say: "The pursuit of abstractions is a good thing, when confined to its proper place. But the breadth of those strains of human character with which *economics* [my italics] is concerned has been underrated by some writers on economics in England and other countries; and the German economists have done good by emphasizing it."[45] Both Pareto and Marshall felt that purely economic abstractions in themselves were not adequate as representations of the concrete environment. Marshall's empiricism led him to feel that this was a serious shortcoming, while Pareto maintained that abstractions allowed deeper analytical insight and hence understanding by way of the long chains of deductive reasonings of which Marshall was so suspicious.

From a scientific point of view, Marshall's "applied sociology" was marred by the introduction of ethical judgments. In his concrete descriptions of "activities" he was preaching a personal ethic. He made pronouncements on what ought to be rather than on what was. Marshall was not alone; I have already pointed to the ethical aspects of other authors' works in the preceding chapter. What is important here is that when writers turned to the consideration of social phenomena—as they had to do when dealing with concrete problems—they were unable to remain detached observers.

43. Parsons, *Structure,* p. 173.
44. Marshall, *Principles,* p. 781. Some indication of Marshall's empiricism is given by the following:
It is obvious that there is no room in economics for long trains of deductive reasoning; no economists, not even Ricardo, attempted them. (*Ibid.,* p. 781.)
If we shut our eyes to realities we may construct an edifice of pure crystal by imaginations, that will throw side lights on real problems; and might conceivably be of interest to beings who had no economic problems at all like our own. Such playful excursions are often suggestive in unexpected ways: they afford good training to the mind: and seem to be productive only of good, so long as their purpose is clearly understood. (*Ibid.,* p. 782.)
45. *Ibid.,* p. 783. Here Marshall is indicating his tolerance for the German historical school's critique of the abstract nature of English economic theory.

PARETO ON THE THEORY OF SOCIAL POLICY

We have seen in the above discussion that Pareto strongly
defended the necessity of abstractions such as *"homo oeconomicus,"*
"homo ethicus," "homo religiosus," and the specialized scientific disciplines which they represented. However, he was appreciative of the
fact that concrete phenomena will always contain properties outside
the scope of a particular specialized science. For this reason, Pareto
was emphatic in stating over and over again that a "synthesis" or integration of the theories of the separate disciplines had to take place
in order to arrive at better "approximations" to human society:
"When one turns from the abstract to the concrete it is necessary to
gather freshly the parts, which for the scope of the study were dis-
joined. Political economy does not have to consider morals, but he
who proposes a practical provision is obliged to take account not
only of economic results, but also of those moral, religious, political,
etc. Science is essentially analytical, practice essentially synthetical."[46]
To the "synthesis" of all specialized disciplines dealing with the
study of human society, Pareto gave the name *sociology.*[47] Pareto admitted that his definition was very inadequate, but he felt that it
could be improved upon in only a small way since strict definitions
were difficult, even in the physical sciences where the subject matter
could be more easily divided for specialized study.
One might ask, how does Pareto's definition of *sociology* differ
from the German view of the "unity of social life"? As concerns the
scope in terms of subject matter, there is little difference. For it appears that Pareto, realizing the interdependence of social phenomena,
was attempting to arrive at a unified social science by a route different from that taken by the German historical school. The crucial difference between the two is one of method. The physical scientists realized the necessity of "analysis" in studying the various aspects of
"concrete" phenomena. This necessity arose because of the inability
of individuals to deal simultaneoulsy with all aspects of concrete phenomena. According to Pareto, this necessity was still not grasped by
many people in the social sciences.[48] As a first step, specialized disciplines, which dealt with certain aspects of human society, allowed
deeper analytical insight and hence understanding by way of long
chains of deductive reasonings. As a second step, Pareto maintained

46. Pareto, *Manuale,* chap. i, sec. 35, pp. 61-62.
47. Pareto, *Mind and Society,* I, sec. 1, p. 3.
48. *Ibid.,* sec. 32, p. 19.

that the *theories* of the specialized disciplines were to be integrated by "synthesis" to form a *sociology* which would render a better *approximation* to human society.[49] But such a synthesis would only be an *analytical* approximation (in contrast to the alleged German *description* of "reality"), since he maintained that we could never have a complete view of the concrete whole.[50] In Pareto's case one tries to grasp the totality of the *forces* at work. In the German case the interest is in the observable totality itself.

Pareto went beyond a mere advocacy of the "synthesis" of the theories of specialized disciplines. In the *Trattato* he undertook such a synthesis—his social equilibrium theory. The "elements" that constitute his system are five: (1) psychological factors, which he called "residues"; (2) human reasonings, which he called "derivations," the most important of which are ideologies; (3) "interests," largely economic; (4) "social heterogeneity," which took account of the individual or group differences in a society; (5) "class circulation," which took account of social mobility in a society. He indicated the elements by letters, as follows: residues, a; interests, b; derivations, c; social heterogeneity and circulation, d. He then considered the ways in which (I) a acted upon b, c, d; (II) b acted upon a, c, d; (III) c acted upon a, b, d; and (IV) d acted upon a, b, c. He devoted the greater part of Chapter XII of the *Trattato* to this task.[51]

To go into the many illustrations and observations that Pareto made in his analysis of the interdependency of the above elements would be beyond the scope of this study. However, certain interesting points of methodological significance do emerge, and these shall be discussed. One very important observation made by Pareto was that each of the "elements" considered by itself yielded a theoretical equilibrium very different from that which was derived from combining all the elements:

The state of concrete equilibrium observable in a given society is a resultant of all these effects, of all these actions and reactions. It is therefore different from a state of theoretical equilibrium obtained by considering one or more of the elements a, b, c, d instead of considering all. Political economy, for instance, deals with category b, and one of its branches is pure economics. Pure economics yields a theoretical equilibrium that is different, still within category b, from another the-

49. *Ibid.,* sec. 34, p. 20.
50. *Ibid.,* sec. 33, p. 19.
51. Pareto, *Mind and Society,* IV, sec. 2206-2395, pp. 1542-1727. Pareto's sociological analysis was essentially qualitative, partly as a consequence of his dealing with qualitative social phenomena rather than with quantitative economic phenomena.

oretical equilibrium yielded by applied economics; and different from other theoretical equilibria that could be obtained by combining *b* with some of the elements *a, c, d*; and different, again, from the theoretical equilibrium that most nearly approximates the concrete and is obtained by combining all the elements *a, b, c, d.*[52]

Pareto was critical of "many literary economists" who failed to understand that different equilibria could result depending on which "elements" were considered. In a rather long footnote,[53] he argued that many economists were inclined to consider the "cycle" of the interdependencies of *bc-cb* exclusively. That is to say, from the study of "interests," *b*, they drew conclusions, *c*, and imagined that economic activity, *b*, could be modified by disseminating the doctrine, *c*. Such was the case of the desirability of free trade. From the study of the economic situation, *b*, was derived the "demonstration," *c*, of its desirability. The *doctrine, c,* of free trade, having gained acceptance, was then used in an attempt to modify the economic situation, *b,* by making free trade a reality. But, in general, when economists encountered "sentiments," *a*, these were assumed to exist independently of economic considerations. If they had considered such "sentiments" seriously—as Pareto felt they were obliged to do when dealing with concrete problems—they would have derived a different "demonstration" regarding theoretical equilibrium.

Pareto recognized Marx as a writer who had noted the existence of a relation between *a* and *b*, and who had thus come "close to a logico-experimental result."[54] According to Pareto, Marx made the "error" of mistaking the relation between *a* and *b* as one of *cause* and *effect*. That is to say, he saw the economic situation, *b*, as the cause acting upon "sentiments," *a*, the effect. Pareto would have been more correct if he had viewed Marx's economic determinism as relation (II) above, i.e., *b* acting upon *a, c, d*. For Marx saw not only "sentiments" but also ideologies and heterogeneity as being affected by material interests.[55]

The "elements" that comprised Pareto's system were psychological,

52. *Ibid.,* sec. 2207, p. 1543. Notice that Pareto feels that a better *approximation* to the concrete is obtained by combining the elements of *a, b, c, d*. We will recall that Pareto argued that all one could hope for in science are better and better approximations to concrete reality, but never a complete picture.
53. *Ibid.,* sec. 2207, n. 1, pp. 1543-44.
54. *Ibid.*
55. Cf. Karl Marx, *Manifesto of the Communist Party* (Chicago: Kerr, 1888), sec. 1, pp. 12-32. See also: Karl Marx, *A Contribution to the Critique of Political Economy,* trans. N. I. Stone (New York: International Library Publishing Co., 1904), Appendix, secs. 1, 2, pp. 265-69, 291-92.

political, economic, and sociological. These were subsumed under the more general concept of social equilibrium. The Paretian theories embodied in each of these elements admittedly have their limitations when viewed from the modern perspective. Recall, though, that during Pareto's time such modern specialized disciplines as social psychology, political science, physical and cultural anthropology, and sociology did not exist. Many apparently qualified writers have been so concerned with the limitations of each of the elements contained in Pareto's system that they have either overlooked or ignored what it was that Pareto had as a primary goal: a study of the reciprocal relation of these elements in their determination of social equilibrium.[56]

Pareto's achievement, and hence his contribution to methodological thought, lies in his systematic and rigorous demonstration that each of the theories dealing with specific areas of action yielded a theoretical equilibrium very different from when they were taken together. A synthesis of the theories of the specialized disciplines was absolutely

---

56. Max Millikan, "Pareto's Sociology," *Econometrica*, IV (Dec., 1936), 326, claims that Pareto sets out to study man's "non-logical" conduct, and that Pareto does not set up anything like a complete explanation of the forces that determine the nature and operation of society. This argument is as absurd to the student of Pareto as an analogous argument which would claim that Pareto's economics was interested in studying man's rational behavior rather than economic equilibrium. Pareto's *assumption* of non-logical behavior is an important factor in certain elements that determine the social equilibrium. Millikan's error is repeated, although to a lesser degree, by Franz Borkenau, *Pareto* (London: Chapman and Hall, 1936), who discusses the *elements* that determine the social equilibrium but completely ignores the social equilibrium that Pareto is aiming to explain. Again, to use an analogy in economics, Borkenau's study would be the equivalent of studying Pareto's "utility" and "production" theories and completely ignoring the general equilibrium analysis under which the two are integrated. In fact, one is rather surprised to find that many discussions of Pareto's sociology end with a rather superficial treatment of the elements or, at times, some of the elements of social equilibrium. The fault partly lies with Pareto himself for the poor writing and organization of the *Trattato*. The fault partly lies with careless reading on the part of many who seem to have become so intrigued with Pareto's sparkling passages that they have lost hold of the theoretical strand woven through the fabric of the four volumes. Also, Pareto seems to be writing as an economist turned sociologist, and he continues to use such terms as "ophelimity," "utility," "maxima," and "index," and to employ the concepts of marginalism, equilibrium, etc. which would be unintelligible to individuals without economic training. The last volume, in which he discusses social equilibrium and social utility using three-dimensional diagrams and speaking of surfaces and planes, etc., would be beyond the capacity of those without specialized training, and this probably accounts for the ignoring of the heart of Pareto's system by many sociologists. More recent writers seem to be more appreciative of this aspect of Pareto's sociology. Cf: Joseph Lopreato, "A Functionalist Reappraisal of Pareto's Sociology," *American Journal of Sociology*, LXIX (May, 1964), 639-46.

essential in order to achieve a better approximation to concrete reality.

To economists, Pareto presents the image of a great economic theorist, and of course this is correct. But the economics profession, in general, has ignored his sociology. Perhaps this is because economists have felt that sociology is outside the scope of economic science.[57] From a purely scientific point of view, in investigating *what is,* this attitude is perhaps correct; for problems must be solved one at a time, and specialized researches have contributed greatly to the knowledge of human society. However, when one turns to questions of economic policy, it seems that the profession has failed to recognize the significance of Pareto's methodological contribution. For Pareto, the idea of *economic* policy as a rule was erroneous; for in order to deal with practical cases it also becomes necessary to take into consideration the non-economic aspects of man's behavior—ethical, political, religious, etc. Pareto believed that the mutual dependency of social phenomena was such that to speak of "policy" was to imply *social* policy. He argued that before economists could speak of policy, they had either to expand the scope of their positive researches to include non-economic phenomena, or to supplement economic theory with the theories of other social science disciplines dealing with non-economic phenomena.[58]

Pareto's methodological views on social policy are gaining greater acceptance among some fields of economics, although the approach is somewhat different (i.e., economists have been reluctant to make economics a sub-branch of sociology). For example, we know today that the notion of "economic" development is meaningful only within the framework of social and cultural development. W. Arthur Lewis makes this point quite clear in the following:

The field of analysis which we have thus set out [economic growth] is customarily said to be divided out between different branches of the social sciences, but if the division has ever been made it has never been effective. Some economists have gone on to study institutions. However, such interests ceased to be fashionable in the second quarter of the twentieth century, and were even authoritatively stated not to be the proper business of economists. All the rest of the field belongs to sociologists, to historians, to students of beliefs, to lawyers, to biologists

57. Some recent writers have ventured into the quicksands of sociology—Schumpeter is an example.

58. Some modern econometric models account for the interdependency of social (or, for that matter, all "non-systemic" variables) phenomena by the introduction of certain "stochastic" variables, whose magnitudes depend on some integral probability law. These stochastic variables become an integral part of the theory, exactly like any other variables.

or to geographers, but they have done little more than to look at it. . . .
One suspects that the sociologists have left the study of economic institutions to the economists, while the economists have left the subject
to sociologists.[59]

It is true that the development of the social sciences has shown a
greater and greater specialization, so that the possibility of synthesis
is much more remote today than in Pareto's time. Precisely the same
problem exists in the physical sciences; through interdisciplinary
co-operation, however, physical scientists have been able to accomplish impressive results.[60]

Unqualified analogies between the physical and social sciences may
be misleading. Ethical neutrality, as mentioned earlier, is often (in
general, but not always) more easily attainable in the physical sciences than in the social sciences. Assuming that the social scientist
could remain a detached observer, other serious problems still remain.

With matters of public policy pertaining to the physical sciences,
practical aims are clearly identifiable (as with our "space program").
Once the aims are known the *technical* problem of choosing the appropriate means remains to be solved. At first glance, the practical
problems of economic science seem to have a striking similarity.
Given the ethical aim of a community, positive economics will provide the alternative means for achieving that aim. If economists accept, as a norm, the efficient allocation of resources, then the choice
of means is reduced considerably. Hence, on the matter of practical
problems there does exist a similarity—or so it seems—between positive economics and the physical sciences. Unfortunately there are

59. W. Arthur Lewis, *The Theory of Economic Growth* (Homewood, Ill.:
Irwin, 1955), p. 12. Lewis' views are, in my opinion, also extensible to the
study of all concrete economic institutions. Even if we choose as a definition
that "economics is what economists do," the fact remains that, in general,
economists (with the exception of the economic sociologists mentioned earlier)
have tended to ignore the intimate relationship between economic and non-
economic phenoma in their studies. An important exception, as I have
mentioned above, is the field of public finance, which borrows heavily from
sociology and political science along Pareto's exhortations.
60. Witness the successes of the National Aeronautics and Space Administration's program, which draws from almost every facet of biological and
physical scientific knowledge. Perhaps my choice of the "space program" is not
the best example, since it pertains to applied fields. Nevertheless the "space
program" involves the question of public goals in the same way that "economic" policy does. In this sense the analogy is useful, especially for what
follows in the text. Another example is the collection of studies known as
"operations research," which draws from a wide range of topics such as linear
programming, input-output analysis, econometric models, game theory, statistical inference, etc.

circumstances that destroy the efficacy of this simple analogy. Take for instance, the economic norm of efficiency.

The economics profession, in general, has chosen as one of its norms the efficient allocation or utilization of resources. Does this imply that society should pursue this norm as an end (assuming that such a goal could be adequately defined)? Not necessarily, for it may be the case that a policy based on the efficient allocation of resources requires certain changes within the structure of society which are in conflict with the non-economic norms obtaining in that society. Where "correct" economic policy would strive for greater efficiency, "correct" social policy would require less efficiency in such cases. Again we are brought back to the problem discussed above: "correct" economic policy and "correct" social policy very often will not correspond.[61] The supporters of the classical doctrine of free trade were advocating a "correct" economic policy, which failed to correspond to "correct" social policy. This argument has been presented several times thus far, and I need not go further into it. What is important is that historically, in choosing their policy norms, economists have often failed to consider the interdependency of social phenomena.

Pareto's methodological views on the interdependency of social phenomena find their most important illustration in his "welfare" theory. In economics a whole field has developed around the "welfare" implications of economic theory. The main concern in welfare economics has been with the development of a criterion for making *economic* welfare judgments. Here again, the limitation lies in the rather restrictive nature of the notion of "economic" utility in comparison to "sociological" utility.[62] This problem will be discussed in detail below.

ECONOMIC AND SOCIOLOGICAL UTILITY THEORY

My main purpose in this section is to illustrate how Pareto's methodological views on the interdependency of social phenomena (with its implications for the scope of economics and sociology) influenced his "welfare" theory. The discussion in this section will also serve to support my position that a failure to understand an author's

61. Admittedly the incompatibility of a policy "mix" may arise in the physical sciences as well.

62. In current usage, "social utility" often refers to the sum total of individual "economic" utilities. But the term "social" utility has an entirely different meaning for Pareto. The distinction will be made clear in the text below.

views on scope and method often results in a failure to understand the doctrines (or theories) themselves. I have in mind specifically the meaning that Pareto attached to such concepts as "utility" and "ophelimity."

Schumpeter has said that even more definitely than being the patron saint of the modern theory of value, Pareto is the patron saint of the "New Welfare Economics."[63] It should be quite clear by now that Pareto strongly advocated the study of what *is* rather than what *ought to be* in economic science, or, as taught today, "positive" economics rather than "normative" economics. Up to Pareto's time what has come to be known as "welfare" economics was intimately related to the utilitarian conception of society. Utilitarian "welfare" doctrines—like the doctrines of any other reform movement—were based on normative principles. Yet, Pareto's name is connected to what was up to his time a normative branch of economics! The irony of the matter is that Pareto became involved in the issue by setting out to show that in a strictly objective sense, very little can be said about economic welfare judgments.

Before going into Pareto's "welfare" theory, it will be necessary to distinguish between Paretian terms and the terms in current usage. Pareto analyzed various meanings of "satisfaction" by differentiating according to the sources of the sentiment and the subjects to whom reference is made. The latter aspect is an indication of the scope of his terminology. The table below summarizes these meanings, together with the Paretian terms that express the concepts and the current terms that are applicable.[64]

I shall not elaborate on the distinctions shown in the table in any great extent. To do so would involve going into Paretian "utility" theory, which is extremely complex and beyond the purpose of this study. What matters here is the distinction between "social utility" as Pareto uses the term and "social utility" as the term is used today. The point is that we do not make this distinction in our usage— rather, we tend to apply the same term (social utility) to concepts for which Pareto had different terms, which leads to confusion. In what follows I shall use the term only in the Paretian sense. Also, I shall use the term "ophelimity" to mean satisfactions derived only from economic causes, in contradistinction to (Pareto's) "utility," which

---

63. Schumpeter, *Quarterly Journal of Economics,* LXIII, 163.
64. The table is the consequence of my own research into Paretian "ophelimity" and "utility" theory. To my knowledge, no writer has ever distinguished the subject and causes of satisfactions in Pareto's theory. In fact, economists have completely overlooked the less subtle distinction between Pareto's "ophelimity" and "utility" theories.

means satisfactions derived from all causes, economic and non-economic. Once these distinctions are kept in mind, what follows can be presented with little difficulty.

I shall begin with brief mention of the state of "welfare" economics before Pareto came on the scene. Regardless of where one looks in the literature of "welfare" economics, be it the English utilitarians or Gossen or Marshall and Edgeworth,[65] one is still confronted with the same obstacle: in current terms, since the satisfactions of individuals are heterogeneous things, they cannot be summed up into a "social welfare function," or to use other words, one encounters the problem of "interpersonal comparisons of utility." Now Pareto, more than anyone else, thought that the idea of "homogeneous ophelimities" in economics was "erroneous" and set out to construct a value theory that dispensed with such concepts. Because individual "ophelimities" were "heterogeneous" in Pareto's view, he felt that interpersonal comparisons of the "ophelimities" of individuals could not be made. However, Pareto came to the rescue: he said that there was in "pure" economics a very restricted criterion by which to make welfare judgments, a criterion which did not involve interpersonal comparisons of "ophelimity." This criterion has become known as the Pareto Optimum. Let us follow his thoughts carefully, ignoring completely any preconceptions we may possess regarding the modern ideas that have become associated with his name.

Pareto argued that to get a more exact picture, one has to state just what norms one intends to follow in determining the "entities" that one is trying to define. He maintained that in "pure" economics, the single norm with respect to value theory was the individual's satisfaction.[66] He reasoned that the maximum of "ophelimity" of a community was not the simple summing of the single individuals' satisfactions, because they were "heterogeneous" quantities and "a sum of such quantities is a thing that has no meaning: there is no such sum, and none such can be considered."[67] The problem then, as Pareto saw it, was to reduce those quantities to "homogeneous"

---

65. I can here only refer to some of the works of these authors: Jeremy Bentham, *An Introduction to the Principles of Morals and Legislation* (1st ed., 1789; Oxford: Clarendon Press, 1907); J. S. Mill, *Utilitarianism* (London: Longmans, Green, Renle, & Dyer, 1867); H. H. Gossen, *Entwickelung der Gesetze des menschlichen Verkehrs* Berlin: R. L. Prager, 1927); Alfred Marshall, *Principles of Economics* (1st ed. 1890; 8th ed.; London: Macmillan & Co., 1925); Francis Y. Edgeworth, *Mathematical Psychics* London: Kegan Paul & Co., 1882). Pareto was thoroughly familiar with the works of these writers.

66. Pareto, *Mind and Society,* IV, sec. 2110, p. 1458.

67. *Ibid.,* sec. 2127, p. 1465.

Table 1. Pareto's Terms and Terms in Current Usage

Pareto's Term	Current Usage	Reference	Source of Satisfaction
1. Individual ophelimity	Personal utility	Individual	Economic
2. Community ophelimity	Social utility	Any group of individuals, but without consideration of collective apart from individual interest	Economic
3. Individual utility	Personal utility	Individual	Any source
4. Social utility	Social utility	Any group of individuals, but without consideration of collective apart from individual interest	Any source
5. Utility of society	Social utility	Any structurally integrated group, with consideration of collective apart from individual interest	Any source

magnitudes (indices of welfare). This of course he did in his ordinal welfare theory.[68] Pareto's argument can be presented in terms of an Edgeworth box diagram.

For simplicity, I shall assume a two-person pure-exchange economy where individuals I and II possess an initial endowment of two goods. The dimensions of the rectangle below represent the total available quantities of Q_1 and Q_2.

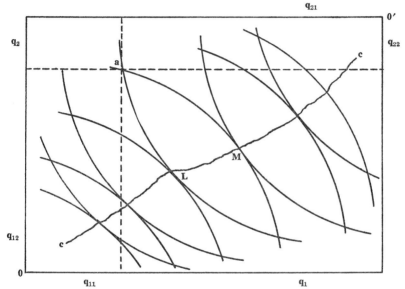

Since the rates of commodity substitution are unequal at point *a*, it is possible to increase the "ophelimity" levels of both individuals by a redistribution of goods, Q_1 and Q_2. If the final position, after redistribution, is between L and M, both individuals will have gained, since both are on higher indifference curves than at point *a*. However, if the final point is *at* L or M, one individual will have gained without any loss to the other individual's position. Once a point on the contract curve (cc) is reached, it is not possible to improve the position of either individual without loss in the position of the other.[69]

68. *Ibid.,* sec. 2128, pp. 1465-66. For a mathematical exposition of the ideas expressed by Pareto, see: Vilfredo Pareto, "Il massimo di utilità per una collectività in sociologia," *Giornale,* XLVI (April, 1913), 337-38. This important article has generally been overlooked in the literature on Pareto.

69. It might be worthwhile to distinguish between what is objective economics and what is distributional in welfare theory. Movements from *a* to L or M contain distributional aspects, as do movements along the contract curve. Only movements to L and M determine how to distribute gains from efficiency improvements, given an initial position more or less "just."

For my purposes, I need only mention that within the assumed frame of reference, a movement *toward* the contract curve always represents an unambiguous improvement of aggregate welfare, but a movement *along* the contract curve alters the distribution of aggregate welfare among the individual participants. According to the conditions of Pareto optimality, any point between L and M is unambiguously superior to point *a*. However, the evaluation of alternative points along the contract curve involves interpersonal comparisons of "ophelimities." According to Pareto, welfare evaluations of movements along the contract curve involve interpersonal comparisons of "ophelimity" (some persons better off, others worse off) which cannot be made from a strictly objective economic standpoint. Hence Pareto concluded that as soon as a community reached a point on the contract curve it had to stop.[70]

In short, Pareto put forward an economic "welfare" criterion that did not depend on considerations of cardinal measurements of interpersonal comparisons of satisfaction. He furnished economics with an important criterion, but a restricted one. When the Pareto Optimum is reached, movements from that point involve resorting to considerations foreign to economics, in order, as Pareto put it, "to decide on grounds of ethics, social utility, or something else, which individuals it is advisable to benefit, which to sacrifice."[71] Again we are confronted with the same methodological view that has repeatedly occurred in previous discussions. According to Pareto, whether one discusses free trade, individualistic versus socialistic regimes, or other community "welfare" propositions, one is led to the same argument—strictly economic considerations are inadequate to deal with such problems; one must resort to non-economic considerations.[72]

Economic science can offer no "objective" criterion (i.e., such as

70. Pareto, *Mind and Society,* IV, sec. 2129, pp. 1466-67.
71. *Ibid.*
72. The limitations of the Pareto Optimum criterion are described by Oskar Morgenstern, "Pareto Optimum and Economic Organization," *Econometric Research Program Research Memorandum No. 63* (Princeton: Unpublished, January 24, 1964). (Used with permission of the author.) While Professor Morgenstern discusses many aspects outside the scope of my interest, it seems in some cases that he objects to the strictly economic considerations as being too restrictive and suggests that the criterion should be expanded to include non-economic factors also. At times he seems to be critical of Pareto for not taking these other factors into consideration. Pareto does this in his sociology. If the economics profession has chosen to ignore this part of Pareto's work, the fault does not lie with him. The rather limited scope of welfare economics has been the subject of criticism by other writers also. Cf. Hla Myint, *Theories of Welfare Economics* (Cambridge, Mass.: Harvard University Press, 1948), chap. xi, for a discussion of the views of these writers.

the Pareto Optimum) for dealing with such problems because they transcend economics. This is why Pareto transferred concrete problems to sociology, which deals with political, ethical, etc., as well as "economic" interests[73] at once.[74]

In his sociological discussion, Pareto dropped the term "ophelimity" (economic satisfaction) and spoke of community *"utility."* When speaking of "utility," as the term was used by Pareto, it is important to keep in mind that this has nothing to do with economic "utility" theory as we use the term today—it is a social concept, deriving from ethical, moral, religious, political, etc., as well as economic causes. In fact, Pareto originally made the distinction between "ophelimity" and "utility" to avoid confusion between strictly economic and "sociological" (both economic and non-economic) considerations.[75]

What matters in this section is that Pareto was fully aware of the restrictive nature of the Pareto Optimum criterion of "welfare"; and that any discussions involving movements from this point involve non-economic considerations. In order to deal with such considerations he developed his sociological "utility" theory. The distinction between Pareto's "ophelimity" theory and "utility" theory has gen-

---

73. Pareto excluded "pure" economics from his sociology. But "economic" interests that have social implications are discussed in his sociology.

74. I might mention that Anglo-American welfare economics in general has respected Pareto's limits. An attempt has been made to bypass the "interpersonal comparison of individual utilities" problem of the older welfare economics by introducing the concept of Social Valuation, where some "superman" assigns relative weights to the desires of the individuals in a society. (Cf. Abram Bergson, "A Reformulation of Certain Aspects of Welfare Economics," *Quarterly Journal of Economics,* LII [Feb., 1938], 310-34; Paul A. Samuelson, *Foundations of Economic Analysis* [Cambridge, Mass.: Harvard, 1947], chap. viii.) This view treats "welfare" as a purely ethical concept "welfare" conclusions being deduced only from "ethical" premises which must be given by "superman." What the concept of Social Valuation does, then, is to transfer the problem of measuring individual utilities to another sphere, i.e., ethics (or "sociology," according to Pareto, since he believed that ethics is a part of "sociology"), so that the economic criterion still becomes the Pareto Optimum.

75. The distinction is completely overlooked by T. W. Hutchison (*A Review of Economic Doctrines 1870-1929* [Oxford: Clarendon Press, 1953], p. 226), who claims that Pareto felt that "interpersonal comparisons of utility are not absolutely 'meaningless' or 'illegitimate'"; giving the impression that Pareto's thoughts applied to economics. This is incorrect; the passage that Hutchison quotes (*Mind and Society,* IV, sec. 2135, pp. 1472-73) is in reference to sociology, not to economics. If Hutchison had not dismissed Pareto's use of the term "ophelimity" as an "insignificant" terminological "novelty," he would have avoided this misleading impression. Here is an excellent example of a situation where knowledge of an author's methodology is useful for understanding his doctrines.

erally been overlooked, resulting in some misleading impressions regarding this aspect of his work.

Finally, because of the "interdependency" of social phenomena found in the concrete environment, concrete problems in general fall outside the scope of economic science so that one must rely on non-economic considerations also, placing such problems in the broader realm of sociology.

V Pareto's Methodology and Method in the Social Sciences

In the introductory chapter we saw that the German economists made a distinction between the methodologies of the physical and social sciences. They accused the English economists of adopting physical science's methods which, in their view, were inadequate in explaining "historical reality." In this chapter I shall examine this issue in greater detail. In particular, I shall show that Pareto's contribution to the methodology of the social sciences lay in his realization that no logical distinction existed between the methodologies of the physical and social sciences. Hence, the methods used by physical scientists—i.e., generalizing concepts—were a valid source of scientific knowledge in the social sciences.

Before proceeding any farther, it might be worthwhile to distinguish between the meanings of the terms "methodology" and "method." The two terms are closely related and often confused. By "method" I mean the techniques or procedures used by researchers in their investigations. On the other hand, "methodology" involves the interpretation or "rationalization" of the procedures used by individuals in their investigations. We saw earlier that Comte attempted to "generalize" science. He aimed at creating a "philosophy of the sciences."[1] Weber, too, attempted to "rationalize" the procedures of science, and raised the question: "what is the logical function and structure of the concepts which our science, like all others, uses?" In particular, "what is the significance of *theory* and theoretical

1. Cf. G. H. Lewes, *Comte's Philosophy of the Sciences* (London: George Bell and Sons, 1904), pp. 8-9.

85

conceptualization (*theoretische Begriffsbildung*) for our knowledge of cultural reality?"[2] The discussions in the preceding chapters were concerned with the nature of science, and the scope of economics and sociology. The discussion of methods, although closely related to these issues, was postponed in order to deal with the problem in greater detail. I now take up this task.

THE CRITIQUE OF THEORETICAL GENERALIZATION IN THE SOCIAL SCIENCES

In the preceding chapter we saw that one implication of the "unity of social life" view of the historical school was its emphasis on detailed historical research, in contrast to traditional theoretical economics with its specialized field of research. In that context I discussed Pareto's and Weber's arguments for the necessity of specialized disciplines in the study of human society. I purposely avoided a discussion of an issue closely related to the "unity of social life" view so that it could be taken up in greater detail in this chapter. This issue is the question of the validity of generalizing concepts in the social sciences. For several reasons, which will be given shortly, the historical school made a definite distinction between the methods used in the study of physical and social phenomena. It was argued by some writers of this view that the methods of the physical sciences, particularly the use of generalizations—laws, for example—were not valid in the study of social phenomena.

In addition to the "unity of social life" view, another view—the "anti-rationalist"—was offered as the basis of a distinction between the two types of sciences, and hence of a corresponding distinction between the methods of these sciences. According to Schumpeter, the "anti-rationalist" view stressed "the multiplicity of motives and the small importance of a merely logical insight where human actions are concerned."[3] Actually, the use of "laws" in the social sciences was attacked by the "anti-rationalists" on two grounds. These will

2. *Max Weber on the Methodology of the Social Sciences,* trans. Shils and Finch (Glencoe, Ill.: The Free Press, 1949), p. 85. For Weber, methodology deals with the nature of causation: "We seek knowledge of an historical phenomenon. . . . How is the causal explanation of an individual fact possible . . . ? Whenever the causal explanation of a cultural phenomenon—an 'historical individual'—is under consideration, the knowledge of causal *laws* is . . . a *means*" (*Ibid.,* pp. 78-79).

3. Joseph Schumpeter, *Economic Doctrine and Method,* trans. R. Aris (London: George Allen and Unwin, 1954), p. 177.

be discussed below and will form the context in which to present Pareto's and Weber's views.

One "anti-rationalist" argument in defense of detailed historical research was that generalizing concepts, being rational, were of little value in dealing with "historical reality." This argument found its strongest advocate in Heinrich Rickert.[4] He argued that social sciences should be concerned with detailed historical research and with the avoidance of any "laws," which were the characteristic methods of the physical sciences.[5]

Pareto conceded that very often the "logical explanations" on the part of "actors" regarding their actions were merely rationalizations of "non-logical" conduct. But Pareto believed that the existence of "non-logical" human actions was not a circumstance that prevented the use of theoretical generalizations regarding such actions. Hence, "uniformities" or "laws" could be deduced from empirical observations of human society in the same way as with the study of "natural" phenomena.[6] Weber, on the other hand, argued that conditions were exactly the opposite from those posited by the "anti-rationalist" argument. He felt that not only could both natural and social phenomena be capable of being observed externally, but in addition, the scientist could impute motives to humans and interpret actions and words as

4. Heinrich Rickert, *Uber die Grenzen der naturwissenschaftlichen Begriffsbildung* (1st ed. 1902; 2nd ed. 1913; Tübingen: Mohr, 1929). See also: *Kulturwissenschaft und Naturwissenschaft: ein Vortrag* (Tübingen: Mohr, 1926). Rickert seemed to overlook the fact that events in nature are "non-rational," too. This circumstance does not deny their rational study. Also, he was not aware that even he had to use some type of rational procedure when he dealt with "historical reality." All *unanalyzed* data lack "rationality." In order to give any meaning to "historical reality," it is necessary to select and systematize historical data. The very process of selection and systematization of data involves some rational procedure: generalization, although often implicit, is always present. External observation can reveal "uniformities" in the study of social phenomena as well as with physical phenomena. Thus, generalizations such as "laws" are useful in the study of human society.

5. Rickert's defense of historical "particularism" may seem dated. Yet, even today, Stark uses arguments similar to Rickert's in the former's defense of sociological "particularism." Stark dichotomizes the social and physical sciences also: "Vainly have the greatest social philosophers, from Vico to Max Weber, pointed out that one kind of science cannot possibly cover two kinds of reality; that the social world which men have made is different, in essence, and hence a different challenge to the mind in pursuit of knowledge, from the physical world which men have not made; that the social sciences, admittedly inferior in other respects, are superior to the physical sciences in that they can not only 'know about' their object, but also 'understand' it— the naive imitation of physics and physiology goes on." Werner Stark, "In Search of the True Pareto," *British Journal of Sociology*, XIV (June, 1963), 103.

6. In his sociology Pareto gives the name "residues" to such "uniformities."

expressions of these actions.[7] This is precisely what Pareto did in his "theory of non-logical actions": he presented a theoretical interpretation of human actions.[8] Thus with respect to this particular "anti-rationalist" argument, both Weber and Pareto agreed that no *logical* difference existed between both kinds of sciences—generalizing concepts would be useful in both studies.

Another "anti-rationalist" argument in defense of detailed historical research that served as a basis for the denial of the validity of generalizing concepts was that of "free will." "Free will" has been understood in many different ways by different writers in Germany, but the concepts of Roscher and Knies were most common to all.[9] Eduard Meyer best reflected their position when he said that by means of the "empirically given ideas of freedom and responsibility, a purely *individual* factor is present in historical development, which is never capable of being reduced to a formula without annihilating its true nature."[10] Meyer attempted to illustrate the proposition of individual freedom of will by arguing the causal significance of the "individually willed" decisions of particular personalities. These decisions, he argued, arose from causes which were, perhaps, never fully to be discovered. He found it necessary to emphasize freedom of will as a fact of "inner experience," indispensable if the individual was to be responsible for his own voluntary acts. One implication of free will, as he understood it, was that prediction—the possibility of "calculating" with "certainty"—typical of the natural sciences, failed in historical researches. Free will (and chance), then, determined the characteristic irrationality in historical events.[11]

7. Max Weber, *Gesammelte Aufsätze zur Wissenschaftslehre* (Tübingen: Mohr, 1922), p. 67.

8. I am unable to go beyond a mention of this theory because its complexity requires extensive elaboration beyond the scope of this study. (See: Vilfredo Pareto, *The Mind and Society*, trans. and ed. A. Livingston (4 vols.; New York: Harcourt, Brace and Co., 1935), I, secs. 161-249, pp. 87-172.) I need only point out here that Pareto made provision for this argument in defense of historical "particularism," thus denying the validity of this particular "anti-rationalist" view.

9. See Weber on Roscher and Knies: *Methodology*, p. 124.

10. See Weber's critique of Eduard Meyer, *Methodology*, pp. 113-30.

11. Meyer does not seem to have been aware that even the physical sciences do not deal with "certainty," but that all predictions involve probabilities in their empirical application, to take account of the random disturbances. This is also the case with the social sciences. The difference between the physical and social sciences in this case is one of degree of uncertainty, rather than lack of it in one and not in the other. Under these circumstances the argument of free will, which allegedly accounts for the common differences between the physical and social sciences and denies the validity of generalizing concepts in the social sciences, is redundant. The fundamental problem, then, is to

Weber gave the "free will" argument a rather novel twist: "The error in the assumption that any freedom of will—however it is understood—is identical with the 'irrationality' of action, or that the latter is conditioned by the former, is quite obvious. The characteristic of 'incalculability,' equally great but not greater than that of 'blind forces of nature,' is the privilege of—the insane."[12] Weber went on to insist that, on the contrary, conditions were exactly opposite to those seen by the "anti-rationalists": "On the other hand, we associate the highest measure of an empirical 'feeling of freedom' with those actions which we are conscious of performing rationally— i.e., *in the absence of physical and psychic 'coercion,' emotional 'effects' and 'accidental' disturbance of the clarity of judgement* in which we pursue a clearly perceived end by 'means' which are the most adequate in accordance with the extent of our knowledge. . . ."[13] Hence, according to Weber, if the concept of "free will" was relied upon, one might find a closer correspondence of human behavior to rational rather than to non-rational action.

The anti-rationalists argued the alleged characteristic "irrationality" of historical "reality," but they did not systematically analyze the problem of rational and non-rational behavior in its relation to social science. If they had done so, perhaps they would not have rested content in their denial of the validity of generalizing concepts in the social sciences. For instance, Pareto and Weber did go on to analyze the problem of rational and non-rational behavior. In doing so, they were able to point out that the existence of non-rational elements in society did not preclude scientific analysis in the social sciences. Let us go into their analyses in greater detail.

The terms "rational," "irrational," "logical," "illogical," "non-logical," etc., all possess an element of vagueness so that they mean different things to different persons. What was needed, then, was a rigorously defined criterion by which to judge human "actions,"[14] to

---

provide for random disturbances regardless of their source, be it free will or something else. Modern econometric models that take account of stochastic variations represent a definite contribution to scientific methodology in this respect. The stochastic element comes either from a misspecification of the model, or from the basic and unpredictable element of randomness in human responses which can be adequately characterized by the inclusion of a random variable term. See J. Johnston, *Econometric Methods* (New York: McGraw-Hill, 1960), p. 6.

12. Weber, *Methodology*, pp. 113-30.
13. *Ibid.*, pp. 124-25.
14. Pareto and Weber used the terms "action" and "conduct" in the same manner as the term "behavior" is used today.

determine whether they belong in the "logical" or "non-logical" category. In order to accomplish this, Pareto distinguished between two aspects of a phenomenon: "as it is in reality and as it presents itself in the mind of this or that human."[15] The first he called *objective* and the second *subjective*. In his distinction between the objective and subjective aspects of actions, Pareto was merely reiterating what others had already said. For example, Weber linked the "subjective intent of the individual . . . to the means which are regarded as correct for a given end."[16] Weber also observed that "a subjectively 'rational' action is not identical with a rationally 'correct' action, i.e., one which uses the objectively correct means in accord with scientific knowledge."[17] In other words, Weber believed that what is "rational" —with respect to a means-end criterion of rationality—from the subjective view of the actor might not be "rational" from the objective view of scientific knowledge.

Pareto also related the objective and the subjective aspects to those "actions" that use means appropriate to ends and that logically link means with ends, and to other "actions" in which these traits are missing:

The two sorts of conduct are very different according as they are considered under their objective or subjective aspects. From the subjective point of view nearly all human actions belong to the logical class. In the eyes of the Greek mariners sacrifices to Poseidon and the rowing with oars were equally logical means of navigation. To avoid verbosities which could only prove annoying, we had better give names to these types of conduct. Suppose we apply the term *logical actions* to actions that logically conjoin means to ends not only from the standpoint of the subject performing them, but also from the standpoint of other persons who have a more extensive knowledge—in other words, to actions that are logical both subjectively and objectively in the sense just explained. Other actions we shall call non-logical. . . .[18]

Both Pareto and Weber classified various types of social "action," but their emphases and procedures varied significantly. Weber classified "social action" into four types, according to the mode of orientation:

(1) In terms of rational orientation to a system of discrete individual ends (zweckrational), that is, through expectations as to the behavior of objects in the external situation and of other human individuals, making use of their expectation as "conditions" or "means" for the

15. Pareto, *Mind and Society,* I, sec. 149, pp. 76-77.
16. Weber, *Methodology,* p. 34.
17. *Ibid.*
18. Pareto, *Mind and Society,* I, sec. 150, p. 78.

successful attainment of the actor's own rationally chosen ends; (2) in terms of rational orientation to an absolute value (wertrational), involving a conscious belief in the absolute value of some ethical, aesthetic, religious, or other form of behavior, entirely for its own sake and independently of any prospects of external success; (3) in terms of affectual orientation, especially emotional, determined by the specific aspects and status of feelings of the actor; (4) traditionally oriented, through the habituation of long practice.[19]

Weber argued that (3) and (4) above were "borderline" cases of rational "action." He interpreted (2) above as examples of "pure rational orientation . . . , regardless of possible cost" to persons who "act to put into practice their convictions of what seems to them to be required by duty, honour, the pursuit of beauty, a religious call, personal loyalty . . . or the importance of some 'cause' no matter in what it consists."[20] He believed that (1) above was "rationally oriented action." The "rational orientation" of (1) is clear. It is less clear what Weber meant by "borderline" cases when he referred to (3) and (4). What is least clear is his interpretation of (2) as examples of "pure rational orientation." The confusion seems to lie in Weber's failure to incorporate his subjective and objective distinction into his value-orientation classification.

Pareto, on the other hand, went on to classify "non-logical" actions according to their objective and subjective relations.[21] He linked the means-end criterion of rationality directly to subjective and objective aspects. Weber did not seem to go beyond a recognition of subjective and objective aspects, his classifications being concerned only with the means-end criterion of rationality.

Both writers also differed in emphasis. Weber's classification stressed the "rational orientation" of the above social actions, whereas Pareto's classification placed emphasis on the "non-logical" characteristics of such actions. The differences in emphasis reflect the intellectual orientations of both writers. Weber saw capitalism as the very embodiment of rationality.[22] For Weber, corporate bureaucracy was rivaled only by state bureaucracy in promoting rational efficiency.[23] However, Weber's "economic sociology" encompassed a greater scope than did traditional economics, so that he had to account for

19. Max Weber, *The Theory of Social and Economic Organization,* trans. A. M. Henderson and Talcott Parsons, ed. T. Parsons (Glencoe, Ill.: The Free Press, 1947), pp. 115-17.
20. *Ibid.*
21. Pareto, *Mind and Society,* I, sec. 151, p. 78.
22. Max Weber, *From Max Weber: Essays in Sociology,* trans., ed., and intro. by H. H. Gerth and C. Wright Mills (New York: Oxford, 1946), p. 49.
23. *Ibid.*

the "depersonalization" of the individual which took place in the process of rationalization. Rationality in this context was seen as adverse to personal freedom.[24] According to Gerth and Mills, although the principle of rationalization is the most general element in Weber's philosophy of history, he saw in rational impersonality a conflict with the quest for individual freedom identified with the "irrational" sentiment of privacy.[25] So in Weber's "economic sociology" account was taken of both the rational and the irrational aspects of human actions. Pareto simply separated the "economic" and "non-economic." In the former he saw "logical" actions predominant, in the latter, "non-logical" actions. Therefore in his sociology he was free to concentrate on the non-logical aspects of human behavior. His conception of non-logical conduct in his sociology did not mean that he denied the importance of rational behavior in human society. He merely constructed two separate scientific edifices—economics and sociology—which dealt with different aspects of concrete social behavior.

What is important here is that both Pareto and Weber presented a highly sophisticated analysis of the problem of rational and nonrational behavior in its relation to social science. In doing so, they were able to show that, contrary to the arguments of "free will," the existence of non-rational elements in society did not preclude scientific analysis. Nor did non-rationality destroy the efficacy of rational procedures, i.e., generalizing concepts, in the social sciences.[26]

Also, Pareto felt that there was no necessity at all to reconcile philosophical arguments of "free will" with certain "uniformities" revealed by observation. He simply looked upon "free will" as a metaphysical concept transcending the limits of his investigation, namely, "logico-experimental" science.[27] Weber, although taking issue with the implications of the "anti-rationalist" argument of "free will," correctly concluded—as did Pareto—that "introducing the philosophical problem of 'freedom' into the procedures of history would suspend its character as an empirical science."[28]

In the introductory chapter I made allusions to a branch of German social theory that placed emphasis on the philosophy of history. The principal names connected with the philosophy of history, according to Weber, were Ranke, Wundt, Munsterberg, Lipps, and Simmel, as

24. *Ibid.,* p. 50.
25. *Ibid.,* p. 73.
26. I shall deal with the Marxian sociology of knowledge in another context below.
27. Pareto, *Mind and Society,* I, sec. 96, p. 51.
28. Weber, *Methodology,* p. 123.

well as Croce in Italy. This branch favored the interpretation of human behavior in terms of a *Geist*. A *Geist* served as a unifying concept, so that its function approximated that of the generalizing concepts used in the physical sciences. However, the *Geist* was applied only to the social whole, rather than to the parts of the whole, in keeping with the organistic orientation of these writers. Parsons observes that the methodological dogma of this view involved the main proposition: " 'generalization' can only mean a grasp of cultural totalities in all their uniqueness, and this grasp takes the form of immediate 'intuition'—a direct grasp of meaning without the intervention of concepts in any form."[29]

Both Pareto and Weber attacked the method of "intuition," as a source of scientific knowledge, through a number of arguments. Weber maintained that "intuition" might uncover causal interconnections—but not generalizations and reflections of "rules."[30] Perhaps Weber went too far in accusing Ranke of "divining" the past when the latter argued that the advancement of knowledge is poorly served if the historian does not possess this "intuitive" gift.[31] However, he did admit that "intuition" in the form of "flashes of imaginations" played an important part in the knowledge of historical relations. It should be pointed out that "intuition" does not account for the common differences between the physical and social sciences, as Ranke seemed to suggest. Intuition is not limited only to knowledge of historical relations, but is generally true of knowledge in the physical sciences.

Pareto was willing to concede less to the value of "intuition" than Weber:

The facts among which we live have their influence upon us, and as a result our minds acquire certain attitudes which must not be too violently in conflict with those facts. That influence—nothing very definite, to tell the truth—of the facts upon our minds makes up such truth, experimentally speaking, as there is in theories ascribing a scientific status to intuition. Intuition serves about as much toward knowledge of reality as a poor, sometimes very poor, photograph of a place serves toward knowledge of that place. Sometimes intuition supplies just a fanciful illusion, and not even a poor photograph of reality.[32]

However, there is a more fundamental scientific problem associated with "intuition." The method of "intuition" presents a problem

29. Talcott Parsons, *The Structure of Social Action* (York, Pa.: McGraw-Hill, 1937), p. 586.
30. Weber, *Methodology*, p. 175.
31. *Ibid.*, **p. 176.**
32. Pareto, *Mind and Society*, I, secs. 108 and 108 n. 1, p. 56.

of "intuitional judgments" that depart farther and farther from "reality." That is to say, "immediate experience" is not capable of precise formulation, so that immediate certainty of perception of meaning must be checked by reference to a rationally consistent system of concepts if "intuitional judgments" are to be avoided. The interpretation of immediate intuitions requires a rational system of theoretical concepts in order to shut the door to uncontrolled and unverifiable allegations. "Intuitional judgments" involving such allegations were, according to Pareto, metaphysical exhortations lacking the critical proof of "logico-experimental" science.[33]

Weber maintained that the advocates of the method of "intuition" confused the "psychological course of the origin of scientific knowledge and 'artistic' form of presenting what is known."[34] Continuing in his words:

We assert nothing at all about the psychologically interesting question which does not, however, concern us here, namely how does an historical hypothesis arise in the mind of the investigator? We are concerned only with the question of the logical category under which the hypothesis is to be demonstrated as valid in case of doubt or dispute, for it is that which determines its logical structure. The dry approach of logic is concerned only with this skeletal structure for even the historical exposition claims "validity" as "truth."[35]

By considering Weber's arguments regarding the logical unimportance of psychological origins of propositions, we are led to a closely related issue concerning the sociology of knowledge. The task of the sociology of knowledge is the precise description of the way in which certain social factors influence certain mental productions.[36] My concern with the sociology of knowledge, at this point, is primarily in the problem of the origins of propositions as concerns their validity. In Marx's sociology of knowledge, the interest-bound nature of ideas was put forward in his attempt to bring "ideological" phenomena into correlation with "material" interests of economic and political order.[37] For Marx, ideas were merely "rationalizations" or

33. *Ibid.,* IV, sec. 42, p. 23.
34. Weber, *Methodology,* p. 176.
35. *Ibid.*
36. For discussions concerning the sociology of knowledge see: Emile Durkheim, *The Rules of Sociological Method* (Glencoe, Ill.: Free Press, 1938); Sidney Hook, *From Hegel to Marx* (London: Gollancy, 1936); Karl Mannheim, *Essays on the Sociology of Knowledge* (New York: Oxford, 1952); Jacques Maquet, *The Sociology of Knowledge* (Boston: Beacon Press, 1951); Weber, *From Max Weber.*
37. Cf. Mannheim, *Essays,* p. 143; Weber, *From Max Weber,* p. 48.

defenses of certain interests and desires.[38] He refused to disassociate historical ideas from material interests. According to Sidney Hook, Marx believed that if history revealed a "progressive" course, it did so only because the historical ideas that triumphed were bound up with definite historical class interests.[39] For Marx, ideas were powerless in history unless they were fused with material interests. Contrary to Weber, the social origins of ideas were important for Marx, since the latter was quick to see a correspondence between ideas and interests. In Weber's early works, there is hardly ever a close connection between interests (or social origin of, say, a speaker or of his following) and the content of the idea during its inception and reception.[40] But as time passed he came to appreciate the weight of material interests in the success of ideas. Finally he wrote: "Not ideas, but material and ideal interests directly govern man's conduct."[41] According to Gerth and Mills, although Weber tended to drift towards Marx, he was engaged in a "fruitful battle" with historical materialism throughout his life.[42]

Pareto was less willing to take Weber's extreme position in the latter's attack on historical materialism. Pareto merely recognized that there were several aspects by which to consider propositions. For the purposes of his own studies in economics, Pareto discounted the importance of psychological (and other) origins of a proposition, concentrating on the "objective" aspect—"not by the manner in which it has been conceived, but by the verification that can be made of it."[43] Nevertheless, he did not ignore the "subjective" or "utility" aspects of a proposition in his sociology. By "subjective" aspects of propositions, Pareto was referring to persons who produce such propositions and to persons who assent to them (derivations). The "utility" aspect of a proposition refers to the "state of mind, the sentiments, that it reflects" (residues).[44] The "objective," "subjective," and "utility" aspects of propositions were extensible to society at large as well as to the individual.[45]

It is interesting to note that although Weber considered himself a follower of the German historical intellectual tradition,[46] he and

38. Cf. Maquet, *Sociology*, p. 6.
39. Hook, *From Hegel to Marx*, p. 122.
40. Weber, *From Max Weber*, p. 63.
41. *Ibid.*
42. *Ibid.*
43. Pareto, *Mind and Society*, IV, sec. 2397, pp. 1727-28.
44. *Ibid.*
45. *Ibid.*
46. Weber, *Methodology*, p. 12.

Pareto were critical—for similar reasons—of its unwillingness to accept the use of theoretical generalizations. The closeness of Pareto's and Weber's views did represent a definite convergence towards a logical meeting ground for traditional economic theory and the historical school's later members. However, the generalizing concepts that both writers defended and expounded were different in that they were conceived within the framework of the respective traditions of both writers. For Pareto, these concepts took the form of "laws"; for Weber, they took the form of "ideal types."[47] These distinctions require further elaboration.

PARETO AND WEBER ON THE STRUCTURE AND FUNCTION OF GENERALIZING CONCEPTS IN THE SOCIAL SCIENCES: A COMPARATIVE ANALYSIS

Although Pareto and Weber were at one in their defense of generalizing concepts, they differed sharply in their views regarding the structure and function of these concepts. Weber believed, for reasons which will be given shortly, that analytical generalizations, such as "laws," were inadequate for social science researches. Instead he proposed the use of "ideal types." Weber's "ideal type" concepts are extremely important in the development of methodological thought. They represented the last formidable barrier to the realization that not only does no formal distinction exist between the physical and social sciences, but also, the structure and function of the generalizing concepts used in both sciences are alike. For that reason I shall devote some considerable space to the analysis of Weber's "ideal types." In contrast to Weber, Pareto saw no formal distinction between the physical and social sciences. This circumstance allowed him to use *analytical* generalizations. I shall show below that his views properly pertain to the general methodology of science.

Weber's economic sociology rested on imposing theory on historical patterns. History is not a social science, but offers data to the social scientist. For example, the intricate task of *The Protestant Ethic and the Spirit of Capitalism* was to explain, causally, the emergence of an "historical individual" (in this instance, modern capitalism).[48] His concern was with the explanation of a particular historical event in its relationship to general or universal propositions. His ap-

47. In the section below I shall point to the significance of Pareto's position in relation to today's accepted view.

48. Max Weber, *The Protestant Ethic and the Spirit of Capitalism,* trans. T. Parsons (London: George Allen & Unwin, 1930).

proach to the study of society differed from "historicism" with its emphasis on the description of "total reality." Hence, Weber's works represent a departure from the traditional methodology of the "older" historical school, reflecting his continued long-standing, self-clarifying polemic against "historicism."[49]

Pareto's distinction between economics and sociology caused him to distinguish between the sources of data of the two disciplines. Nevertheless, for Pareto, too, history offered data to the sociologist. However, the generalizations derived from historical data differed for the two authors. These differences, and the methodological bases for them, will be discussed below.

We have seen that Weber did not agree with the arguments of the historical school regarding the distinction between the natural and social sciences. On the other hand, Weber did maintain that such a distinction was valid on other grounds. According to Weber, scientific interest in social phenomena lay in the "understanding of the characteristic uniqueness of the reality in which we move."[50] Also, "social science attempts to understand the relationships and cultural significance of *individual* events in their contemporary manifestations, and the causes of their being historically *so* and not *otherwise*."[51] Thus Weber strongly emphasized the causal explanation of the *historical uniqueness* and *concrete individuality* of social phenomena as a subject of study. In fact, by Weber the term "historical" (but not "history") was treated as synonymous with individuality: "we seek knowledge of an historical phenomenon, meaning by historical: significant in its peculiarity (*Eigenart*)."[52] Here we see a definite link with the historical school. On the other hand, Weber argued that the natural sciences looked for "universally valid" propositions, such as "laws," which were important and valuable to those sciences as "ends in themselves."[53] He felt that the very universal characteristics of "laws" made them "devoid of content" and least valuable for the "knowledge of historical phenomena in their concreteness."[54] Finally, he concluded that the thesis which stated that "the ideal of science is the reduction of empirical reality to 'laws' is meaningless" in in the social sciences.[55] Weber then advanced what he believed to be

49. For Weber's critique of "historicism" see: *Methodology,* pp. 113-64.
50. *Ibid.,* p. 72.
51. *Ibid.*
52. *Ibid.,* p. 78. Some examples of Weber's "historical individuals" are capitalism, the Indian caste system, etc. In this connection I might note that there are few, if any, Weberian economists, only economic historians. The latter tend to isolate and emphasize the economic aspects of history.
53. *Ibid.,* pp. 80, 86.
54. *Ibid.,* p. 80.
55. *Ibid.*

the basic methodological distinction between the two types of sciences: in the natural sciences, formulations of universal generalizations are adequate as *ends* in themselves; in the social sciences, at the very most, if at all, they can only be a preliminary *means* to the elucidation and understanding of "historical uniqueness" and "concrete individuality." Hence, theoretical concepts cannot stand in the same relation in both sciences. Weber was never able to remove himself entirely from the influence of the Kantian dichotomy between the physical and social sciences.

Pareto, although not disputing the "historical uniqueness" and "concrete individuality" of particular historical events, argued that abstraction allowed the study of "uniformities" which were found among many different historical events. This view is crucially different from Weber's "individual uniqueness" argument. Pareto, unlike Weber, was not interested in rendering causal explanations of *particular* "historical individuals," in his initial approximations. His interest in history was only in so far as it furnished the data, in the form of many historical events, from which to derive general "laws" of society. Let us examine Pareto's own words:

Little or nothing can be inferred directly from mere description and in that sense the apothegm that "history never repeats itself" is very true. Concrete phenomena have to be broken up into ideal phenomena that are simpler, that we may arrive at something more nearly constant than the complex and ever shifting thing we have before us in the concrete. That "history never repeats itself" identically is just as certain as it is that history is "always repeating itself" in certain respects that we may call main respects. It would be inconceivably absurd to imagine that history could produce an event identically repeating the Peloponnesian War, in the sense of being an exact copy of it. But then again, history shows that that war, which arose in the rivalry between Athens and Sparta, is only one item in an endless series of similar wars that have been brought on by similar causes, that in that sense there are numberless copies of it that are likenesses, to some extent at least, of the wars that arose in the rivalries between Carthage and Rome down to all the other wars that have been fought in all periods of history then and now.[56]

In other words, both physical and social scientists are seeking to find "experimental uniformities" which may even be called "laws."

56. Pareto, *Mind and Society,* IV, sec. 2410, pp. 1735-36. In Pareto's sociology the "laws" that Pareto derives from historical data are for the most part "psychologically" oriented "laws" of human behavior, which "explain" human conduct from antiquity to modern civilization. These "laws" he calls "residues." They are much more general in their applicability than Weber's "ideal types."

For Pareto, "experimental uniformities" were a preliminary *means* in both sciences for the elucidation and understanding of concrete "reality." In this sense "not the slightest [functional] difference arises between social laws and physical laws."[57]

I shall now discuss the generalizing concepts incorporated into the systems of the two authors. Weber's theoretical concept focused upon his theory of the "ideal type." This concept is rather difficult to present clearly, because he failed to distinguish several types of concepts included under the term. It is perhaps best to begin by taking up Weber's distinction between the natural and social sciences. It will be recalled that Weber argued in favor of the use of theoretical concepts in both kinds of science. The basic distinction between these two kinds of science, as he saw it, required different types of "generalizing" concepts. Weber posed the question: "What is the logical function and structure of the concepts which our science, like all others, uses?"[58] To these concepts, which for him were peculiar to the social sciences, Weber gave the name "ideal type." What is the "ideal type"? Weber seemed to be more clear on what it is not.[59] To use Parsons' words:

(1) It is not a hypothesis in the sense that it is a proposition about concrete reality which is concretely verifiable, and to be accepted in this sense as true if verified. In contrast to the sense of concreteness, it is abstract. (2) It is not description of reality if by this is meant a concretely existing thing or process to which it corresponds. In this sense also it is abstract. (3) It is not an average . . . in the sense that we can say the average man weighs 150 pounds. This average man is not an ideal type. (4) Nor, finally, is it a formulation of the concrete traits *common* to a class of concrete things, for instance in the sense that having beards is a trait common to men as distinct from women. . . .[60]

I can best give meaning to Weber's "ideal types" through analyzing their function and structure in Weber's own works. Weber included as "ideal types" two heterogeneous categories: "generalizing" and "individualizing" types. "Individualizing ideal types" consisted of two groups: (1) concrete "historical individuals,"[61] such as bourgeois capitalism, the Indian caste system, etc., and (2) "ideas,"[62] such as Calvinistic theology, Brahmanic philosophy, etc. The "individualizing ideal types" constituted the *objects* of causal analysis. Their function

57. *Ibid.*, I, sec. 99, pp. 52-53.
58. Weber, *Methodology*, p. 85.
59. See *ibid.*, pp. 90, 101.
60. Parsons, *Structure*, p. 604. The above discussion of Weber's "ideal types" relies on Parsons, *Structure*, pp. 604-7.
61. Weber, *Methodology*, pp. 91-93.
62. *Ibid.*, pp. 94-96.

was to provide typology, categories, etc., to concrete material in preparation for causal analysis. The "individualizing ideal types" were not "explanations" but only "objects" which were to be "explained." The "generalizing ideal typical" concept is the category in which I am most interested. The "generalizing ideal type" is the concept that Weber used in place of generalizations such as "laws," which he believed were not valid in the social sciences.[63] Again using Parsons' words, it can best be described as: ". . . an ideal construction of a typical course of action, or form of a relationship which is applicable to the analysis of an indefinite plurality of concrete cases, and which formulates in pure, logically consistent form certain elements that are relevant to the understanding of several concrete situations."[64] Examples of the "generalizing" kind of "ideal typical" concept which Weber used were "handicraft," "individualism," "bureaucracy," "church," and "sect."[65] These examples were "ideal" only in the sense of being constructions with a fictitious simplification and exaggeration of certain features, according to Weber.[66] They are hypothetically concrete entities, a state of affairs or a process or a unit in one of these.[67] The "generalizing" kind of "ideal type" requires all the characteristics given above: (1) hypothetical concrete entity, state of affairs, process, or unit; (2) abstract generality; (3) fictitious simplification or exaggeration of empirical reality. The first without the second might apply to a single historical event, in which case it would not be a general concept. The first without the third might make it a common trait or statistical average, characteristic of the "laws" used in the natural sciences.

The "individualizing ideal type" and the "generalizing ideal type" concepts are interrelated in Weber's system. Since the number of data is so great and the question of relevance is complex, it is necessary to construct an "historical individual" which is the thing to be explained, according to Weber.[68] The process of description involves

63. I have not been able to find any evidence that Weber's reasons for using "generalizing ideal types" were partly the consequence of his dealing with qualitative social phenomena rather than quantitative economic phenomena. We shall see below that Weber's "generalizing ideal types" stem from his attempt to explain "historical individuals."

64. Parsons, *Structure,* p. 606.

65. Weber, *Methodology,* pp. 93, 101. Weber's failure to distinguish explicitly between "individualizing" and "generalizing" types caused him to "lump" all "ideal types" together, with the result of ambiguity. Alexander von Schelting, *Max Weber's Wissenschaftslehre* (Tübingen: Mohr, 1934), was the first writer to distinguish between the functions and structures of the two concepts.

66. Weber, *Methodology,* p. 90.

67. Weber called such hypothetical concrete entities "utopias" (*ibid.,* p. 90).

68. *Ibid.,* p. 75.

referring parts of it to type concepts beyond the range of applicability of the particular case.[69] Hence Weber, in discussing the "historical individual" of "modern capitalism," used the "generalizing" concept of "bureaucracy."

It is clear that the bureaucratic organization of a social structure, and especially of a political one, can and regularly does have far-reaching economic consequences. But what sort of consequences? Of course in any individual case it depends upon the distribution of economic and social power, and especially upon the sphere that is occupied by the emerging bureaucratic mechanism. The consequences of bureaucracy depend therefore upon the direction which the powers using the apparatus give to it. And very frequently a crypto-plutocratic distribution of power has been the result.

. . . .

In modern times bureaucratization and social leveling within political, and particularly within state organizations in connection with the destruction of feudal and local privileges, have very frequently benefited the interests of capitalism. Often bureaucratization has been carried out in direct alliance with capitalist interests, for example, the great historical alliance of the power of the absolute ruling prince with capitalist interests. In general, a legal leveling and destruction of firmly established local structures ruled by notables has usually made for a wider range of capitalist activity.

. . . .

The bureaucratic structure is everywhere a late product of development. The further back we trace our steps, the more typical is the absence of bureaucracy and officialdom in the structure of domination. Bureaucracy has a 'rational' character: rules, means, ends, and matter-of-factness dominate its bearing. Everywhere its origin and its diffusion have therefore had 'revolutionary' results, in a special sense, which has still to be discussed. This is the same influence which the advance of *rationalism* in general has had. The march of bureaucracy has destroyed structures of domination which had no rational character, in the special sense of the term.[70]

In other words, the "generalizing" concept "explains" the "historical individual." A final step—not important to my purposes, but one which Weber included—involves the formulation of typical lines of development for these "types."[71]

I have already mentioned the methodological basis for Weber's defense of the use of generalizing "ideal types." His argument in defense of generalizing "ideal types" was dubious, since in the natural sciences, formulations of generalizations are not only *ends* in themselves. They are also means. Also, his argument is superfluous if no

69. *Ibid.*
70. Weber, *From Max Weber,* pp. 230, 244.
71. *Ibid.,* p. 76.

distinction is made as to degrees of abstract construction. Both generalizing "ideal types" and "laws" are theoretical generalizations. "Laws" are merely "higher level" abstractions. Weber was correct in his observation that the very universal characteristic of "laws" made them "devoid of content" when compared to "ideal types." But this circumstance alone should not make them "least valuable" for the "knowledge of historical phenomena in their concreteness."

Pareto's ideas regarding the *structure* of "generalizing" concepts differed greatly from Weber's, since Pareto did not distinguish between degrees of abstract construction. Instead he used *analytical* generalizations in his researches. An *analytical* generalization—a concept which Weber discussed also—is a general concept relating to the totality of concrete entities included in a class and formulated according to common traits or statistical averages, as in the natural sciences. These take the form of what are commonly known as "laws" (Weber: "social laws" and "natural laws") or, to use Pareto's term, class "uniformities." But Weber's distinction between the natural and social sciences precluded the use of *analytical* generalizations in the social sciences. He had to use the "ideal type" generalizations, since the "historical individual" to which this "type" is applied is an "historically unique" phenomenon of which *class* concepts of the above kind cannot be adequately descriptive—at least in Weber's view.

We have seen that Pareto, in contrast to Weber, recognized no formal basis for the distinction between the natural and social sciences. This circumstance allowed him to take full advantage of the methodological achievements of the physical sciences in their application towards the study of social phenomena. In fact, he often presented examples from the physical sciences—particularly in his economics—scrupulously pointing out that they were merely analogies, not identities. It may be said that Pareto's views properly pertain to the general methodology of science, since he made no logical distinction between the function and structure of generalizing concepts in the natural and social sciences. For Pareto, then, the generalizing concepts used in the study of social phenomena were of the same type as those used in the physical sciences.

More recently, Carl G. Hempel has attempted to explicate the methodological character of typological concepts and to appraise their potential significance for the purposes they are intended to serve.[72] He points out that although many uses of "type concepts" are

---

72. Carl G. Hempel, "Typological Methods in the Social Sciences," in *Science, Language, and Human Rights* (American Philosophical Association, Eastern Division, Philadelphia: University of Pennsylvania Press, 1952), pp.

by now of historical interest only, some branches of research, especially psychology and the social sciences, have continued to employ such concepts. He adds, that for social science, the use of ideal types has been declared one of the methodological characteristics that distinguish it essentially from natural science. In his study Hempel analyzes many type concepts, in addition to Weber's "ideal types." Significantly, he reaches conclusions similar to those of Pareto: "In sum, then, the various type concepts in psychology and the social sciences, when freed from certain misleading connotations, prove to be of exactly the same character as methods of classification, ordering, measurement, empirical correlation, and finally theory formation used in the natural sciences. In leading to this result, the analysis of typological procedures exhibits, in a characteristic example, the methodological unity of empirical science."[73] In other words, the modern view in the philosophy of science is that, formally, the function and structure of generalizing concepts used in the physical and social sciences are alike—a position taken by Pareto over half a century ago.

65-86. Also reprinted in Maurice Natanson (ed.), *Philosophy of the Social Sciences: A Reader* (New York: Random House, 1963), pp. 210-30.
    73. *Ibid.*, p. 230.

VI Pareto's Methodology and Method in Economics

INTRODUCTION

INTRODUCTION

In the last two chapters, we saw that a controversy developed between the writers who were more interested in qualitative and descriptive research and those who stressed quantitative and analytic work. The methodological basis for the controversy has been discussed in some detail. I now turn to economics proper. In economics, a similar controversy occurred between the "literary" and the "mathematical" economists. During the nineteenth century, a mathematized form of theory developed which became known as the "new" economics. The principal names connected with this development were Cournot, Walras, Edgeworth, Fisher, and Pareto. To say the least, a great deal of confusion existed regarding the role of mathematics in economics during Pareto's time. In this chapter I shall analyze the basis for Pareto's defense of mathematical methods in economics. In his defense of the "new" economics Pareto was the first economist to clarify the issues involved in the controversy.

The nineteenth century also witnessed the application of statistical methods and testing in economics. Pareto's researches in this field were a pioneering achievement in what later became known as econometrics. He attempted the numerical determination of certain functions, based on observation of factual data, although he did not include an indication of the confidence intervals to certain numbers. Statistical researches were also attacked by the "literary" economists. I shall show in this chapter that Pareto's contribution consisted in a better understanding of the interplay of theory and empirical work.

Finally, some attention will be given to the criterion for accepting or rejecting theories, namely, the "verification problem" in economics. The "verification problem" focuses attention on the veri-

104

fication of the explanatory or predictive value of hypothetical generalizations, a problem which Pareto recognized and wrote about.

PARETO ON MATHEMATICAL METHODS IN ECONOMICS

The use of mathematical methods has been criticized, for one reason or another, throughout the history of economics.[1] The German historical economists, who were antagonistic towards economic theory for methodological reasons, saw in mathematical economics a further extension of the "mechanistic" orientation of traditional theory. Even Menger and the Austrian economists, who were much more tolerant towards economic theory than were the Germans, objected to the use of mathematics on methodological grounds. We have seen that Menger, for example, thought that mathematical analysis deprived economic phenomena of their qualitative "essence." In England, even Marshall, as we shall see below, seems to have had mixed feelings about the use of mathematics in economics. In this section I shall contrast Marshall's and Pareto's views, since Marshall was the leading "literary" economist.

Marshall thought that mathematical analysis was "unrealistic." In discussing the mathematical economics of Jevons, Walras, Pareto, and Fisher, he singled out Fisher as an illustration:

The writings of Professor Fisher contain a masterly argument, rich in fertile suggestion, in favor of a comprehensive use of the term [capital]. Regarded from the abstract and mathematical point of view his position is incontestable. But he seems to take too little account of the necessity for keeping realistic discussions in touch with the language of the market place; and to ignore Bagehot's caution against trying "to express various meanings on complex things with a scanty vocabulary of fastened uses."[2]

Marshall's main criticism of mathematical economics was that this form of theorizing was beyond the grasp of most "literary" econ-

1. For a recent criticism of mathematical methods in economics, see: David Novick, "Mathematics: Logic, Quantity and Method," *The Review of Economics and Statistics,* XXXVI (Nov., 1954), 357-58. In defense of mathematical economics, see: P. Samuelson, L. R. Klein, J. Duesenberry, J. Chipman, J. Tinbergen, D. Champernowne, R. Solow, R. Dorfman, T. Koopmans, Postscript by the Editor, "Mathematics in Economics: Discussion of Mr. Novick's Article," *Ibid.,* pp. 359-86. A recent discussion of the role of mathematics in the social sciences is found in: James C. Charlesworth (ed.), *Mathematics and the Social Sciences, The Utility and Inutility of Mathematics in the Study of Economics, Political Science and Sociology,* A Symposium, sponsored by The American Academy of Political and Social Science (Philadelphia: June, 1963).

2. Alfred Marshall, *Principles of Economics* (1st ed. 1890; 8th ed.; London: Macmillan & Co., 1925), p. 788.

omists, as well as the general public. He called attention to the apparent need for a prose translation of a mathematical argument so that a larger group could benefit from the work done by a few mathematical economists.[3] Marshall's dictum presented two problems for economic science. Firstly, it required that those who use mathematics apply the additional effort to restate a mathematical theory in literary form. Also, Marshall seemed to imply that mathematics is a language, which, as with other languages, can be "translated" into prose language without loss.[4] The assumption seems to be that mathematics is merely a simplified (symbolic) form of prose language, hence allowing for a more rigorous exposition.[5]

In contrast to Marshall, Pareto felt no necessity "for keeping realistic discussions in touch with the language of the market place." He left this task to others.[6] Also, Pareto argued that many people thought that the chief advantage of mathematics consisted in making a demonstration more rigorous. He believed this to be an error,[7] for, according to Pareto, a demonstration that is well constructed by ordinary methods of logic is just as rigorous as one made by the application of mathematical logic. The chief advantage of mathematics in deductive researches, he maintained, is that mathematics makes it possible to express relations between facts which are not possible with other facilities or ordinary language.[8] Since the value of mathematics in such cases lies in its use as a logical tool, Pareto referred to this form of mathematical reasoning as "unnumerical" mathematics, a term used by Edgeworth.

3. Today, Marshall's argument is repeated by Novick, *Review of Economics and Statistics,* XXXVI, 358.

4. In his *Foundations,* Samuelson maintained that mathematics is a language. On the other hand, R. Dorfman, *Review of Economics and Statistics,* XXXVI, 375, disagreed with Samuelson and stressed the importance of mathematics as a logical system. Later Samuelson reconciled Dorfman's apparent disagreement by saying, ". . . as to the sense in which mathematics is a language [the difference] will evaporate once it is realized that I regard logic as a language in exactly the same sense" (*ibid.,* p. 280 n. 21). These distinctions will be elaborated upon in connection with Pareto's views in the text.

5. More recently, Champernowne, *Review of Economics and Statistics,* XXXVI, 370, in his defense of mathematical methods, indicates that this view still prevails among some critics of mathematical economics.

6. Many of Pareto's theories were "translated" to prose form by his contemporary, Philip Wicksteed, *Common Sense of Political Economy* (London: Routledge, Kegan Paul, 1933).

7. Vilfredo Pareto, "The New Theories of Economics," *The Journal of Political Economy,* V (Sept., 1897), 490-91.

8. Vilfredo Pareto, *Cours d'économie politique* (2 vols.; Lausanne: Librairie de l'Université, 1897), I, sec. 559, n. 4, pp. 476-77.

Many were critical of the use of mathematics in deductive studies for many reasons in addition to those given by Marshall, although Pareto took great pains to explain the limitations and possibilities of such methods in the *Cours*. Finally he felt compelled to write in defense of mathematical economics, in answer to the many criticisms of his *Cours*. We will recognize in the following passage a sophisticated defense of a mathematized form of theory in "pure" economics:

> Certain critics cry out apodictically against the new theories as being absurd because they attempt to state economic phenomena 'in mathematical formulae.' But no such pretentious attempt has been made. These critics may therefore be told that, far from aiming to express complex phenomena in simple formula, economists broadly avow that they do not know of any concrete phenomena in all its details. They are solely acquainted with ideal phenomena which make a continually closer approximation to concrete cases.
>
> Pure economics has no better way of expresssing the concrete economic phenomena than rational mechanics has for representing the concrete mechanical one. It is at this point that there is a place for mathematics. The problem of pure economics bears a striking likeness to that of rational mechanics. Now, in point of empirical fact, men have as yet not succeeded in treating the latter problem without the aid of mathematics. It therefore appears quite legitimate to appeal also to mathematics for assistance in the solution of the economic problem.
>
> The advantage of mathematics lies chiefly in this, that it permits us to treat problems far more complicated than those generally solved by ordinary logic. Most economists insist upon the mutual dependence of different economic phenomena. But a purely verbal recognition of this fact is not all that can be done or all that is required. What we want is to determine, at least approximately, the relations existing between the economic phenomena under discussion and so obtain a clear conception of their interdependence. A system of equations similar to the one used in mechanics to represent the equilibrium and the movement of bodies is afforded by this method of approximation. This representation is, no doubt, in this way approached in a rough way at best, and yet the approximation serves better than nothing.[9]

In the above citation we see that Pareto uses the physical sciences as an analogy in his defense of mathematical economics. We saw in an earlier chapter that Pareto made no *logical* distinction between the physical and social sciences, in that his views on scientific methodology pertained to all sciences. Since he made no logical distinctions between the sciences he was allowed to take, freely, advantage of the mathematical achievements of the physical sciences.

Notice that in the above citation Pareto argues that an important

9. Pareto, *Journal of Political Economy*, V, 489-91.

advantage of mathematical logic is that it allows for a systematic study of the interdependency of economic phenomena. This is an extremely important aspect of Pareto's methodology: he stressed the analysis of the "mutual dependence" of economic phenomena as well as the "mutual dependence" of *social* phenomena. These considerations require further elaboration.

Pareto was thoroughly familiar with Marshall's partial equilibrium analysis and thought it to be very useful. He felt that Marshall was prudent with regard to the implications of his partial analysis. However, Pareto believed that the "Marshallians" overlooked the limitation of studying economic units in isolation. They often ignored the mutual dependencies of the economic phenomena whose analysis mathematical economics permitted.[10] At bottom, the underlying issues are those of causal relations and functional interdependencies. Let us examine Pareto's thoughts:

There are various ways of envisaging interdependent phenomena. Suppose we classify them: 1. Relations of cause and effect, only, may be considered, and interdependence wholly disregarded. 2. Interdependence may be taken into account: 2a. Relations of cause and effect are still considered, but allowance is made for interdependence by considering actions and reactions, and by other devices. 2b. One may work directly on the hypothesis of interdependence. The soundest method, undoubtedly, is the one we designate as 2b. . . .[11]

Pareto explained his choice of 2b above by arguing that in "reality" we observe interdependent economic units, acting and reacting upon each other. He argued that, in the early development of economics, the tools to deal with the complexities of interaction were lacking. Economists had to rely on "ordinary" logic to study only simple relations of cause and effect. Economic units were analyzed in "isolation." With the introduction of mathematical logic to economic analysis, the mutual dependencies of economic units could be studied—at least in a theoretical manner.[12]

---

10. However, he did attack Marshall's assumption of a constant utility of money since it did violence to the facts. See: Vilfredo Pareto, *Manuale d'economia politica* (Milano: Società editrice libraria, 1906), Mathematical Appendix.

11. Vilfredo Pareto, *The Mind and Society,* trans. and ed. A. Livingston (4 vols.; New York: Harcourt, Brace and Co., 1935), III, sec. 1732, pp. 1192-93.

12. Pareto, *Manuale,* chap. iii, sec. 3, p. 143. This is not to say that mutual dependencies cannot be studied without mathematical methods. For instance, history treats interdependencies too. But very complex systems are easily handled when relations can be expressed mathematically—the Walrasian general equilibrium model, for instance.

Of course, Walras' equations of general equilibrium represented a pioneering effort in the study of the interdependency of economic phenomena. Pareto defended the Walrasian tradition of general equilibrium analysis. His reasons were methodological. We recall Pareto's concern with the fragmentation-of-knowledge problem. He felt that, in order to achieve a closer approximation to concrete reality, a "synthesis" should take place through which all aspects of concrete phenomena—economic, ethical, political, etc.—would be treated simultaneously. The same methodological argument is applied to economics: "it becomes absolutely necessary to consider them [individual economic units] as a whole after having examined them in isolation."[13] His reason for supporting the functional interdependency concept is that the concept avoids errors of attributing to certain phenomena causal relationships which are highly "unrealistic" and "unscientific." Continuing with one of his examples:

> If one thinks in terms of tastes [demand], production being given, then the value in exchange is determined exclusively by tastes; and hence, the cause of value is ophelimity. On the other hand, for one who thinks in terms of obstacles [production], the cause of values is the cost of production. If with obstacles one stops to consider only labor, then the cause of value is exclusively in labor. Thus it was with Marx—in his theory of value other conditions were eliminated such that value depended only on labor.[14]

According to Pareto, then, general equilibrium analysis (and other models of more than one equation) avoids errors to which earlier economists were committed when they considered only isolated economic units.[15] What is particularly surprising is that Walras himself

13. Pareto, *Journal of Political Economy,* V, 493.
14. Pareto, *Manuale,* chap. iii, sec. 225, p. 234.
15. The empirical application of the concept of general equilibrium had to await the availability of the necessary statistics. Wassily Leontief, "Interrelation of Prices, Output, Savings and Investment," *The Review of Economic Statistics,* XIX (Aug., 1937), 109-32, was the first notable attempt to apply the concept to empirical analysis. In addition to the lack of statistical data, there is another reason why the interdependence viewpoint of the Lausanne School remained empirically barren, namely, that statistical methods at the time presented limitations for the application of the interdependence concept in empirical work. All this has changed more recently. According to Henry Briefs, *Three Views of Method in Economics* (Washington, D. C.: Georgetown University Press, 1960), the Maximum Likelihood Method of parameter estimation is a specific statistical technique which promotes the maximization of a joint likelihood function with respect to all parameters simultaneously, given the observations of all the jointly dependent and independent variables specified in the model (p. 5). Less technically, it is the statistical counterpart of the Walras-Pareto type of simultaneous equation approach. (Cf. T.

was unable to remove himself from a deterministic view. With respect to Walras, Pareto had this to say: "He [Walras] expresses two contradictory concepts. For one part he says 'all the unknowns of the economic problem depend on all the equations of economic equilibrium.' And this is a good theory. On the other hand he affirms 'to be certain that rareté (ophelimity) is the reason of value of exchange' and this is reminiscent of past theories which do not correspond to reality."[16]

In addition to seeing in mathematics a method for dealing with interdependent relations, Pareto realized that mathematics, as a method of expressing relations symbolically, brought out the formal structure of these relations. In turn, the analysis of the properties of these formal structures could reveal further relationships not perceptible through "ordinary" language.[17] Pareto's general equilibrium analysis provides an excellent example of the advantage of purely formal structures in economic analysis.

In Pareto's system, every individual attempting to satisfy his "tastes"—the "forces" that impel the individual to action[18]—encounters "obstacles." These "obstacles" may be (a) the "tastes" of persons with whom one contracts, (b) limitations of a given quantity of a commodity that must be divided with someone else, (c) the fact that in producing one good, the goods of others may be a necessary part of production, (d) the fact that a good which is desired is not available in time and space, (e) social organization.[19] He dispenses with the traditional divisions of equilibrium analysis such as exchange, production, and distribution. By doing so he lifts the logical core of economic theory from the institutional garb in which it is given, allowing the study of highly simplified formal structures and hence providing greater insight into, and understanding of, the economic equilibrium. Thus the study of economic equilibrium is carried to its highest degree of generality. Pareto was able to show that highly abstract mathematical systems, although "devoid of content,"

Haavelmo, "Quantitative Research in Agriculture Economics: The Interdependence between Agriculture and the National Economy," *Journal of Farm Economics,* XXIX [Nov., 1947], 910-14.) On the other hand, single equation estimation, the statistical counterpart to partial analysis, finds a modern advocate in Herman Wold, *Demand Analysis: A Study in Econometrics* (New York: Wiley, 1953), pp. 50-52.

16. Pareto, *Manuale,* sec. 227, pp. 235-36.

17. Significantly, the arguments have not changed much since Pareto. Cf. Champernowne, *Review of Economics and Statistics,* XXXVI, 370, and R. Dorfman, *ibid.,* p. 374.

18. Cf. Pareto, *Manuale,* chap. iv.

19. *Ibid.,* chap. v.

are extremely important to economic science. As Schumpeter has observed:

The first idea that must occur, from a purely theoretical point of view, to anyone who has mastered Walras' system is to raise it to a still higher level of generality. When we follow Walras and, indeed all the marginal utility theorists on their progress through the phenomena of exchange, production, and so on, we discover that they are trying to solve problems that in ultimate logic reduce to one only: *all* their problems—not only the problems of production—are problems in the transformation of economic quantities formally alike, the differences consisting merely in the different restrictions to which economic action is subject in different fields. Suppose we decide to do what we do in *all sciences* [my italics], that is, to separate out the common core once and for all. This point of view of "mental economy" (E. Mach's *Denkökonomie*) will justify this endeavor to utilitarians. A theory of this kind will work with quite general indices, such as "tastes" and "obstacles." . . . We may transcend economics and rise to a conception of a system of undefined "things" that are simply subject to certain restrictions and then try to develop a perfectly general mathematical logic of systems. Pareto did the same. . . .[20]

Schumpeter also points out that contrary to charges of "arid generalizations" hurled at Pareto's system, such a "logical stone" produced "economic bread." For it was through his abstract model that Pareto discovered that the problems of production in an individualist and in a collectivist state were formally alike (see page 45 above). In this Pareto furnishes us with a concrete illustration of the value of highly abstract mathematical systems, of which Marshall was so suspicious, for the social sciences as well as the physical sciences.

In summary, Pareto presented a highly sophisticated defense of mathematical methods in economics. He was a leader among mathematical economists in clarifying the issues involved in the controversy.[21] Pareto's arguments were very similar, at least in substance, to

20. Joseph Schumpeter, "Vilfredo Pareto (1848-1923)," *Quarterly Journal of Economics,* LXIII (May, 1949), 158.

21. For instance, just about all that Walras had to say (in the *Elements*) in his defense of mathematical economics was put in the form of one question: "As to mathematical language, why should we persist in using everyday language to explain things in the most cumbrous and incorrect way, as Ricardo has often done and as John Stuart Mill does repeatedly in his *Principles of Political Economy,* when these same things can be stated far more succinctly, precisely and clearly in the language of mathematics?" (Léon Walras, *Elements of Pure Economics,* trans. William Jaffé [Homewood, Ill.: Irwin, 1954], p. 72). Of course, I am not suggesting that Walras did not actively campaign for mathematical economics. Nevertheless, he confessed that his main purpose in engaging in politico-economic controversies was to call attention to his analytic work. See: Léon Walras, *Correspondence of Léon Walras and Related Papers,* ed. William Jaffé (3 vols.; Amsterdam: North Holland, 1965), I, 711-12; II,

the recent arguments in defense of mathematical economics by some of the leading mathematical economists today.

Yet even today a recent critic of Pareto, Stark, goes so far as to claim that the use of mathematical "models" by Pareto "inhibited the advancement of our knowledge of economic reality."[22] It is true that Pareto did influence the development of scientific economics, as reflected in modern utility and production theories, as well as welfare economics. However, nowhere does Stark show how Pareto's influence was inhibitory to the advancement of economic science. At bottom, the source of Stark's complaint—although he is never clear in distilling the issues—goes back to the methodological controversy between those who were interested in qualitative and descriptive research and those who stressed quantitative and analytic work.

Writers who stressed qualitative and descriptive researches actually represented two different methodological views. We have seen that some of the German economists, who stressed the "reality" of the cultural totality—economic, political, ethical, and other aspects— were anti-theoretical. They saw in mathematical economics a further extension of the "mechanistic" orientation of traditional theory. The "literary" economists were not anti-theoretical, but they attacked the mathematized form of theory characterized by mathematical economics. Nevertheless, the development of economics, as well as the development of political science and sociology, has witnessed the increasing application of mathematical methods for the analysis of social phenomena which were presumed to be qualitative during Pareto's time.[23]

PARETO ON THE INTERPLAY OF THEORY AND EMPIRICAL WORK

Many of the "literary" economists were not only critical of the application of mathematics to theory; they also argued against the

---

212. As Jaffé has pointed out, "Walras sought to arouse economists to the importance of mathematics as a tool of economic analysis—in an endeavor to convert them to his novel conception of a pure theory of economic equilibrium" (*Ibid.*, I, vii). Hence, Walras' main interest was in popularizing his own work rather than in the methodological basis for his method. The task of rationalizing the procedures of the mathematical economists was left to Pareto. Pareto's article, "The New Theories of Economics," was an extremely important contribution to economic science in this respect.

22. Werner Stark, "In Search of the True Pareto," *British Journal of Sociology*, XIV (June, 1963), 108.

23. Cf. Charlesworth, *Mathematics and the Social Sciences*, for discussions of mathematics in the study of economics, political science, and sociology.

numerical determination of mathematical functions in empirical work. For example, both Cairnes and J. N. Keynes argued the impossibility of obtaining exact numerical premises in economics.[24] J. N. Keynes went so far as to say that Cournot and "other mathematical economists" realized such an impossibility.[25] On the other hand, Marshall, who considered himself a "literary" economist, saw great value in statistical researches.[26]

Apparently J. N. Keynes overlooked Pareto's statistical researches. In fact, it was, according to Schumpeter, "a highly original achievement in econometrics that first established his international reputation and, under the title of 'Pareto's Law,' created what may be fairly called a whole literature devoted to its critical discussion."[27]

In the *Cours* Pareto not only mathematized theory, he also attempted the numerical determination of certain functions, in the form of empirical curves. Yet in the *Manuale* statistical research is almost completely lacking. This circumstance is indeed strange in view of the fact that Pareto felt that the future of economics was in statistical research. Even after the publication of his *Manuale,* Pareto reaffirmed this position: "The progress of political economy depends, in the future, in great part on the research of empirical laws, derived from statistics, which are then compared with the theoretical laws noted, or which from them may be understood new ones. Those empirical laws are in substance given by interpolation of statistical data, from which appears the great importance of such operations."[28] One might ask, then, why did he turn his attention away from statistical researches? Giorgio Mortara feels that it was a question of the inevitable limitations upon the capacity to work which a lifetime imposes upon a person—a matter of priorities—that induced Pareto to devote his later energies in economics to pure theory.[29] Perhaps a likely explanation is the limitation encountered by the lack of statistical data. It is

24. John E. Cairnes, *Character and Logical Method of Political Economy* (London: Macmillan, 1875), p. vii; J. N. Keynes, *The Scope and Method of Political Economy* (4th ed. 1917; New York: A. M. Kelley, 1963), p. 257. Today this argument is repeated by Ludwig Von Mises, *Epistemological Problems of Economics* (Princeton: Van Nostrand, 1960), pp. 116-18; *The Ultimate Foundation of Economic Science* (Princeton: Van Nostrand, 1962), pp. 23, 26, 55, 85.
25. J. N. Keynes, *Scope and Method,* p. 257.
26. Marshall, *Principles,* pp. 781-82.
27. Schumpeter, *Quarterly Journal of Economics,* LXIII, 155.
28. Vilfredo Pareto, "L'interpolazione per la ricerca della leggi economiche," *Giornale,* XXXIV (March, 1907), 266. Pareto did not include an indication of the confidence intervals. This development came later.
29. Giorgio Mortara, "Pareto statistico," *Giornale,* LXIV (Jan.-Feb., 1924), 121.

interesting to note that although Pareto was critical of the methodological views of the German historical economists, he made use of their published statistics and recognized the importance of their work in this respect. Also, statistical methods at the time presented limitations for the application of the interdependence concept in empirical work (see footnote 15 above). Another possible reason why Pareto did not continue with such researches—or, for that matter, with economics in general—may have been his great impatience to get to sociology. As Hutchison has observed: "The *Cours* and *Manuale* are the interim reports of a gigantic intellect, moving impatiently on to ever wider problems, and frequently leaving it to the reader to work out the full significance of the pregnant, concise, but often terminologically untidy hints so profusely scattered in its wake."[30] Pantaleoni seems to confirm this view. He maintains that Pareto's main interest was in sociology from the very beginning. If one relies on Pareto's works as an indication of his interests, however, it would appear that he acquired such an interest in the later part of his career.[31]

Regardless of the reasons, Pareto did not turn away from statistical research without leaving his mark in that field. He wrote several articles in which he presented the results of his research, and he also published articles on statistical methods.[32]

What is important for the purposes of this section is that Pareto's contribution consisted in a better understanding of the interplay of theory and empirical work. He not only defended statistical methods in economics, but was also able to show the efficacy of such methods in his own pioneering work. In addition, his efforts represented a notable contribution to economic science in another way: the success of his statistical researches lent great weight to his methodological stance that there was little basis for the alleged logical distinction between the physical and social sciences. Hence the methods of both

30. J. W. Hutchison, *A Review of Economic Doctrines 1870-1929* (Oxford: Clarendon Press, 1953), p. 218.

31. Maffeo Pantaleoni, "In occasione della morte di Pareto: reflessioni," *Giornale*, LXIV (Jan.-Feb., 1924), 8-13.

32. See, Pareto: "La mortalità infantile e il costo dell'uomo adulto," *Giornale*, VII (Nov., 1893), 451-56; "Il modo di figuari i fenomeni economici," *Giornale*, XII (Jan., 1896), 75-87; "La curva della entrate e le osservazioni dell professor Edgeworth," *Giornale*, XIII (Nov., 1896), 439-48; "Aggiunta allo studio curva della entrate," *Giornale*, XIV (Jan., 1897), 15-26; "Quelques exemples d'application des méthodes d'interpolation à la statistique," *Journal de la Société de statistique de Paris* (Nov., 1897), pp. 367-79; "Tables pour faciliter l'application de la méthode des moindres carrés," *Journal de statistique suisse* (1899), pp. 121-50; "L'interpolazione per la ricerca delle leggi economiche," *Giornale*, XXXIV (March, 1907), 266-85, and XXXVI (June, 1908), 432-53.

sciences were very similar. I shall illustrate the latter point with reference to Pareto's own researches. As examples, I shall discuss his "law" of income distribution and his population theories.

Pareto found that the distribution of income for various countries tended to take the form of a particular curve when plotted as a cumulative frequency function. His income distribution curve, also known as "Pareto's Law," can be cast in the following statement: If we call N the number of income receivers having the income X or greater, A and α being parameters, then the distribution of income is given by the formula:

$$\log N = \log A - \alpha \log X.$$

The issue of whether this income distribution curve is a "law" or not centers on the constancy of α. Pareto found α to be relatively constant using statistical data available to him from such diverse countries as England, Ireland, Germany, Italy, and even Peru.[33] Subsequent empirical studies by others involving different countries indicated α to have only slight average variations of value, and these were within statistical error.[34] Today, this formulation applies to certain parts of the cumulative frequency function.[35] The advantage of the Pareto distribution is that it presents a very convenient formulation for dealing with data involving extremely skewed distributions. For this reason it remains popular, in addition to its original application, for many statistical studies today.[36]

Pareto was very scrupulous regarding his "law." In particular, he said: "This law being empirical, it may not always remain true, especially not for all mankind. At present, however, the statistics which we have present no exceptions to the law; it may therefore provisionally be accepted as universal. But exceptions may be found, and I should not be greatly surprised if some day a well-authenticated exception were discovered."[37] Yet many misunderstandings occurred regarding Pareto's usage of the term "law." Even today, Stark, for example, repeats the old criticisms and the same denials that were

33. For a detailed discussion, see: Pareto, *Cours,* II, secs. 950-89, pp. 327-85.
34. A discussion of the controversy that developed in connection with "Pareto's Law" is presented by N. O. Johnson, "The Pareto Law," *The Review of Economic Statistics,* XIX (Jan., 1937), 20-26.
35. Cf. L. Klein, *An Introduction to Econometrics* (Englewood Cliffs, New Jersey: Prentice-Hall, 1962), pp. 150-54.
36. Cf. Benoit Mandelbrot, "New Methods in Statistical Economics," *Journal of Political Economy,* LXXI (Nov., 1963), 421-40. Pareto's "law" is an "exact" model in which the predictive aspect is stressed while the stochastic aspect is supressed. In this sense it served as a first approximation to later stochastic models.
37. Pareto, *Journal of Political Economy,* V, 501.

made during Pareto's lifetime. He dismisses Pareto's hypothesis with the statement, "the most elementary acquaintance with facts of history proves beyond the shadow of a doubt that this is not so," without presenting any factual evidence in the way of refutation.[38] He claims that one of Pareto's "weaknesses" was that he assumed "that the laws of economics are exactly like the laws of physics: once true, true forever," and points to "Pareto's Law" as evidence.[39] This is simply erroneous; one only need refer to the above citation to see that Pareto believed no such thing. In his criticism of "Pareto's Law" Stark has raised the old polemic, discussed in the preceding chapters, between the historical school and Pareto.[40]

Another important statistical study made by Pareto was that of the relationship between demographic and economic changes ("movements"), in the chapter *Les Capitaux Personnels* of the *Cours*. This chapter contains a wealth of statistical data, mostly on European countries, and occupies about one-fifth of Volume I. He employed three sets of indices to support his inference that population "movements" are related to economic "movements"—mortality, natality, and nuptiality. He found that all of these were related to economic changes, but in varying degrees. Of course, the economic index must be representative of the type of economy if one is to arrive at any significant results; thus Pareto used, as indices, harvest yields and prices of grain for the early part of the nineteenth century. As industrialization progressed in certain countries in the latter part of that century, Pareto found that these indices were less useful; instead, he used exports, imports, bank clearings, and grain prices. He found that for England, marriages and births moved with exports. The correspondence between economic prosperity and marriages, he

38. Stark, *British Journal of Sociology,* XIV, 110.
39. *Ibid.*
40. One is reminded of the anecdote of the encounter between Pareto and Schmoller as told by Livingston in *The Mind and Society:*
"Giving a lecture before the convention of scientists at Geneva, Pareto was interrupted from the floor by a patronizing cry from Gustav Schmoller, an economist of the then German Strassburg: 'But are there laws in economics?' Schmoller had no personal acquaintance with Pareto at the time. After the lecture Pareto recognized his heckler on the street and sidled up to him in his shabby clothes [Pareto was famous for his indifference to the exteriors that go with wealth and fame] and in guise of a beggar: 'Please, sir, can you direct me to a restaurant where one can eat for nothing?' 'Not where you can eat for nothing, my good man,' the German replied, 'but here is one where you can eat for very little!' 'So there *are* laws in economics!' laughed Pareto as he turned away." ("Biographical Note," *Mind and Society,* I, p. xviii).
Pantaleoni also recalls the incident in "In occasione della morte di Pareto: reflessioni," *Giornale,* LXIV, 12-13.

found, was very close in time, while maximum births were achieved after a time lag.

Pareto, not being an economic determinist, was very careful in pointing out that he had not shown the "explicit dependence" of population movements on the economic situation, but merely their dependence on variations in it. He stated that this difference was not clearly understood by persons not trained in mathematics:

> If the economic state is characterized by a function F of a number of variables which are functions of time t, we have demonstrated that the number of marriages, births, and to a certain extent also deaths, are a function of dF/dt; but we have not shown that such numbers are explicit functions of F. . . . Mortality rates are terms which are explicit functions of F. For births and marriages, the changes, which depend explicitly upon F are marked by changes in tastes and habits which depend upon a difference in well-being.[41]

Taking the results of his researches in population and distribution of incomes, Pareto made the following scientific prediction:

> If total income increases with respect to population, [and Pareto's empirical researches indicated that the *rate* of population increase in Europe was diminishing] there must either be an increase in the minimum income, or a decrease in inequality in incomes, or the two must result simultaneously.[42]

We now arrive at a methodological issue discussed earlier. His prediction was interpreted by many as an attack on the popular doctrine of socialism during that time—the social evolution was such that the rich would grow richer and the poor poorer. Pareto's observations were often severely criticized, especially in Germany, because they ran counter to the sentiments of many reformers. Pareto was later able to point out that between 1897 and 1911 there was an increase in total income with respect to population, and what in fact resulted was both an increase in minimum income and a decrease in inequality of income.[43]

Referring to his critics, Pareto reflected that although propositions are often accepted merely because they are "obvious," in accord with one's sentiments, such propositions have no place in "logico-experimental" science. He criticized his own *laissez faire* sentiments, as we have seen in an earlier chapter, for the same reasons.

41. Pareto, *Cours,* I, sec. 180 n. 1, p. 114. For an excellent discussion of Pareto's population theories see: J. J. Spengler, "Pareto on Population I," *Quarterly Journal of Economics,* LVIII (Aug., 1944), 593-98; "Pareto on Population II," *Quarterly Journal of Economics,* LIX (Nov., 1944), 107-33.
42. Pareto, *Cours,* II, sec. 965, p. 361.
43. Pareto, *Mind and Society,* I, sec. 77, pp. 40-43.

I shall now evaluate the significance of Pareto's statistical researches from the point of view of his methodology. We saw earlier that the German historical economists accepted the Kantian dualism between the methodologies of the physical and social sciences. Their acceptance of Kant's observations was reflected in their critique ot traditional economic theory. They argued that the physical and social sciences were *logically* distinct, and hence the application of "methods" of the physical sciences to the social sciences was inappropriate. The Germans, especially Schmoller, were empirically oriented. They collected and published a great deal of statistical data. The crucial difference between Pareto's and the German economists' statistical researches is that Pareto's constructs took the form of equations including a specification in the form of numerical determination of the functions, which he "tested" empirically and from which he made predictions. His procedures were, of course, similar to those used in the physical sciences. Pareto was thus able to show, in a concrete way, that the statistical "methods" of the physical sciences were an important source of scientific knowledge for economics. His pioneering achievements in econometrics lent great weight to his arguments that no *logical* methodological distinction existed between the physical and social sciences. Stark has correctly appreciated the influence of Pareto's economics, and its corresponding methods, upon modern economics. However, what is of paramount importance, at least for the purpose of this section, is this: Pareto displayed a very find comprehension of the interplay of theory and empirical work. Through his distribution-of-income and population researches, he was able to show that the statistical testing of theories was in fact possible, contrary to the views of many "literary" economists.

Of course, Pareto's simple correlation technique was only a first step. Later developments in econometrics gave rise to more sophisticated stochastic models and to the application of statistical inference theory to empirical research.

PARETO ON THE VERIFICATION PROBLEM IN ECONOMICS

For the most part, Pareto's predecessors and contemporaries had little to say about the "problem of verification" in economics.[44]

44. The term "verification problem" was first used in connection with Fritz Machlup's article, "The Problem of Verification in Economics," *Southern Economic Journal*, XXII (July, 1955), 5-6. For the main economic discussions on

J. S. Mill and J. N. Keynes were exceptions. J. S. Mill argued that "to verify the hypothesis itself *a posteriori,* that is, to examine whether the facts of any actual case are in accordance with it, is no part of the business of science at all but of the application of science."[45] He did point out that "we cannot . . . too carefully endeavor to verify our theory, by comparing, in the particular cases to which we have access, the results which it would have led us to predict, with the most trustworthy accounts we can obtain of those which have been actually realized."[46] J. S. Mill seemed to emphasize the predictive value of "theory" (more correctly, hypothesis). He did not propose to put the assumptions of the "theory" to empirical tests. He said "the ground of confidence in any concrete deductive science is not the *a priori* reasoning itself, but the accordance between its results and those of observation *a posteriori.*"[47]

In his famous treatise on methodology, J. N. Keynes hardly went beyond J. S. Mill on verification. He accepted J. S. Mill's observations with only a slight qualification. He pointed out that there might be independent grounds for believing that premises correspond with

---

the problem of verification see: Fritz Machlup, "Operational Concepts and Mental Constructs in Model and Theory Formation," *Giornale degli economisti e annali di economia,* XIX (Sept.-Oct., 1960), 553-82; "The Problem of Verification in Economics"; "Rejoinder to a Reluctant Ultra-Empiricist," *Southern Economic Journal,* XXII (Apr., 1956), 483-93; T. W. Hutchison, *The Significance and Basic Postulates of Economic Theory* (London: Macmillan, 1938); "Professor Machlup on Verification in Economics," *Southern Economic Journal,* XXII (Apr., 1956), 476-83; Milton Friedman, "The Methodology of Positive Economics," in *Essays in Positive Economics* (Chicago: University of Chicago Press, 1953), pp. 3-43; Ludwig Von Mises, *The Ultimate Foundation of Economic Science* (Princeton: Von Nostrand, 1963); Jack Melitz, "Friedman and Machlup on the Significance of Testing Economic Assumptions," *Journal of Political Economy,* LXXIII (Feb., 1965), 37-60; Paul A. Samuelson, *Foundations of Economy Analysis* (Cambridge, Mass.: Harvard, 1947), pp. 3-6; "International Factor-Price Equalization Once Again," *Economic Journal,* LIX (June, 1949), 181-97; "International Trade and the Equalization of Factor Prices," *Economic Journal,* LVIII (June, 1948), 163-84; "Problems of Methodology—Discussion," *American Economic Review, Proceedings,* LIII (May, 1963), 231-36; "Theory and Realism: A Reply," *American Economic Review,* LIV (Sept., 1964), 736-39; Fritz Machlup, "Professor Samuelson on Theory and Realism," *American Economic Review,* LIV (Sept., 1964), 733-36. Also see Melitz, *Journal of Political Economy,* LXXIII, p. 38 n. 6, for other writers who have touched upon the problem of verification.

45. J. S. Mill, *Essays on Some Unsettled Questions of Political Economy* (London: J. W. Parker, 1844), p. 143.

46. *Ibid.,* p. 154.

47. J. S. Mill, *A System of Logic* (London: Longmans, Green & Co., 1884), Bk. VI, chap, ix, p. 620.

the facts "in spite of the fact that there is difficulty in obtaining explicit verification."[48] Then he went on to say:

There must not of course be a manifest discrepancy between our theoretical conclusions and the actual facts. But we should not hastily draw negative conclusions, or suppose theories overthrown, because instances of their operation are not patent to observation. For the complexity of the actual economic world, which in the first place makes it necessary to have recourse to the deductive method, may also render it difficult to determine whether or not the actual effects of any given agency really correspond with the results of our deductive calculations.[49]

Hence, J. N. Keynes was really pointing to the practical problem encountered in testing the predictive value of an hypothesis.

As concerns the matter of prediction, Pareto seemed to agree with J. S. Mill and J. N. Keynes:

No departure from the experimental field and therefore from the domain of logico-experimental theories . . . is involved in the resort to hypotheses, provided they are used strictly as instruments in the quest for consequences that are uniformly subject to verification by experiences.[50]

He added that:

When any considerable number of inferences from a given hypothesis have been verified by experience, it becomes exceedingly probable that a new implication will likewise be verified; so in that case . . . there is a temptation to accept the new inference without verifying it. That explains the haziness present in many minds as to the distinction between hypotheses subordinate to experience and hypotheses dominating experience. Still, as a matter of practice there are cases where the implications of this or that hypothesis may be accepted without proof. For instance, certain principles of pure mechanics are being questioned nowadays, at least as regards velocities to any considerable degree greater than velocities practically observable. But it is evident that the mechanical engineer may continue to accept them without the slightest fear of going wrong, since the parts of his mechanics move at speeds which fall short of any that would require modifications in the principles of dynamics.[51]

However, Pareto went beyond J. S. Mill and J. N. Keynes in one significant respect. Although J. S. Mill and J. N. Keynes stressed the predictive value of hypotheses, they did not specify the conditions necessary for such a "test." In fact, we have seen that J. N. Keynes

48. J. N. Keynes, *Scope and Method,* p. 233.
49. *Ibid.,* pp. 233-34.
50. Pareto, *Mind and Society,* I, sec. 59, p. 28.
51. *Ibid.,* sec. 61, p. 29.

argued the impossibility of the numerical determination of equations, and hence the impossibility of statistical "testing" of hypotheses. Since Pareto was interested in statistical "testing" of hypotheses, he took a different stance. He argued that in order to put an hypothesis to a predictive test, the hypothesis had to be cast in a manner that would allow empirical verification. Now this statement appears rather obvious. But in fact, the marginal utility postulate, as it was conceived by Pareto's predecessors and contemporaries, violated Pareto's requirement. The utility postulate was an expression of the psychological principle of hedonism, a principle which could not be put to an empirical "test." I shall discuss Pareto's critique of the marginal utility hypothesis as an illustration of his views on empirically meaningful hypotheses.[52]

In the *Manuale,* Pareto broke with the marginal utility economists, dropping the concept of marginal utility altogether and employing indifference curves first used by Edgeworth.[53] This does not suggest that in adopting Edgeworth's invention Pareto adopted Edgeworth's utility theory. Those not familiar with the methodological aspects of both writers' works often overlook this point. Whereas Edgeworth started with the assumption of measurable total utility from which he deduced the definition of these lines, Pareto inverted the process. Pareto took the indifference curves as given and showed that it was possible to deduce from them *indices* of welfare. The indifference curves have an entirely different meaning in Pareto's usage because they are divested of the concept of measurable total utility. Hence in Pareto's general equilibrium system it is possible to arrive at equilibrium without the utility postulate. Pareto's achievement, then, is more methodological than technical, because he replaced the empirically barren utility postulate with a postulate about *observable* behavior, i.e., revealed preference, and thus placed economic theory on a more empirically secure foundation. Pareto felt that indifference curve analysis was more "experimental" not because he proposed to find the indifferences and preferences that individuals really possessed, but because it is not repugnant to one's logic to suppose that such a possibility exists.[54] "We have now reached the point where we must

52. I shall also show in the text that Pareto's views came close to Samuelson's "operationally meaningful theorems."

53. Cf. Francis Edgeworth, *Mathematical Psychics* (London: Kegan Paul & Co., 1882). For Pareto's discussion of Edgeworth's use of indifference curves see: *Mind and Society,* IV, sec. 2078, n. 1, pp. 1442-43.

54. Pareto, "Economie Mathématique," *Encyclopédie des Sciences Mathématiques,* Tome. I, Vol. IV, Fasc. 4, (Paris: Teubner, Gauthier, Villars, 1911). Translated into English as: "Mathematical Economics," *International Economic Papers,* V (1955), 69.

look to concrete phenomena as a guidance for our future study. We shall see whether observation can provide us with the data we need. It is not a question, at least for the moment, of realizing such experiences; it will be sufficient to establish their theoretical possibility."[55]

I repeat, although he did not propose to find the indifferences and preferences that individuals really possessed, it was not repugnant to one's logic to suppose that such a possibility did exist. In other words, he replaced the utility postulate with a postulate that could conceivably be "tested" empirically. In doing so, he placed economic theory on a more secure foundation.

Pareto's view on empirically meaningful hypotheses comes very close to present-day scientific standards. For instance, in his *Foundations*, Samuelson stresses the point that Pareto was trying to make. Samuelson argues that few economists have been concerned with "operationally meaningful theorems." He explains:

By a *meaningful theorem* I mean simply a hypothesis about empirical data which could conceivably be refuted, if only under ideal conditions. A meaningful theorem may be false. It may be valid but of trivial importance. Its validity may be indeterminate, and practically difficult or impossible to determine. Thus, with existing data, it may be impossible to check upon the hypothesis that demand for salt is of elasticity —1.0. But it is meaningful because under ideal circumstances an experiment could be devised whereby one could hope to refute the hypothesis.[56]

Both Pareto and Samuelson are firm supporters of a program emphasizing the derivation of empirically meaningful hypotheses. In this, their main concern is with placing economic theory on a more secure empirical foundation.

Pareto's contribution to the "problem of verification" does not end with the above. Pareto saw that the value of an assumption diminishes as its (counterfactual) "unrealism" increases.[57] In other words, the greater the contradictions between assumptions and facts, the greater the possibility that derived hypotheses are not "true."[58] I shall discuss certain aspects of Pareto's works in order to lend substance

55. *Ibid.*
56. Samuelson, *Foundations*, p. 4.
57. In this respect, Pareto represents a point of view supported by Jack Melitz, *Journal of Political Economy*, LXXIII, 59-60, and Samuelson, *American Economic Review, Proceedings*, LIII, 236. Melitz does not, however, link varying degrees of realism of assumptions to the method of successive approximations, as does Pareto; nevertheless, this is not a substantive difference.
58. Here Pareto comes very close to Samuelson's view that a theorem deduced from counterfactual hypotheses cannot yield empirically true consequences (Samuelson, *Economic Journal*, LIX, 181).

to my argument that he believed the value of an assumption to be directly related to its "reality."

Pareto accepted the assumption of rational behavior in economics on the basis of its correspondence to the facts. Also, he went so far as to argue that economics had advanced much farther than the other social sciences because economics dealt with "logical" conduct. With respect to sociology, he argued the "reality" of his assumption of "non-logical" behavior. He claimed that the distinctions he made between "logical" and "non-logical" conduct were not merely hypothetical, but had points of correspondence with "reality." What is important here is that Pareto believed that the "reality" of the assumptions used in economics was important. Pareto spoke of *successive approximations*—the "complication of problems by the introduction of new facts"—which bring theories into closer correspondence with "reality." Since the very purpose of successive approximations was to bring the "pure theories of economics into closer correspondence to reality," it meant that the "new facts" introduced into "pure" theory should have their origin in empirical observation and "experience." For Pareto, the "reality" of the assumptions, introduced into theory with successive approximations, was critical. In fact, the very methodological basis for his critique of Walras' marginal productivity theory involved the question of the "reality" of Walras' assumption.[59]

59. Pareto's critique of the marginal productivity theory is one example of a situation sometimes found in the literature in economics—if one relies on the secondary sources, one can be easily misled if not completely confused. M. Blaug, *Economic Theory in Retrospect* (Homewood, Ill.: Irwin, 1962), p. 408, claims that both Pareto and Walras "continued to insist that conditions approximating to fixed input coefficients of production did occur." This is incorrect. Henry Schultz, "Marginal Productivity and the Pricing Process," *Journal of Political Economy*, XXXVII (Oct., 1929), 521, seems to think that Pareto's reformulation of the coefficients of production meant that Pareto "bade adieu to the marginal productivity theory," an impression which is not entirely without error. John Hicks, "Marginal Productivity and the Principle of Variation," *Economic Journal*, XII (Feb., 1932), p. 86, n. 7, thinks that Pareto's reasons for a "correction" of the marginal productivity theory as given in the *Cours* are "merely silly" and adds that "there is nothing corresponding to it in the *Manuel*," apparently overlooking the fact that there was no need for Pareto to mention his example again because by then he had developed the apparatus to deal with the problem. George Stigler, *Production and Distribution Theories* (New York: Macmillan, 1946), dismisses Pareto's arguments by defending the use of variable coefficients of production *as a first approximation,* seemingly not aware of the fact that Pareto found this perfectly acceptable even as a second approximation. He also completely fails to mention Pareto's more general solution, where the production function is not linear and homogeneous, and instead places reliance on Wicksell, Barone, and Walras. The latter two's solutions are only special cases of Pareto's general solution.

I shall not go into the technical details of Pareto's critique of the marginal productivity theory. Instead I shall emphasize the methodological basis for his critique. The methodological significance of Pareto's reformulation of the Walrasian marginal productivity theory is this: he did not feel that the assumptions of the later Walrasian model, i.e., variable coefficients of production, were adequate to treat the particular problems one encounters in *subsequent approximations*. Pareto simply felt that economic science, like all other sciences, was in a perpetual state of development, and that the assumptions of the older theories should be supplemented by more "realistic" (empirically factual) ones in an effort to bring the science in closer correspondence to concrete "reality." He gave many *concrete* examples of circumstances in which one finds not *only* fixed or *only* variable coefficients of production, but both fixed and variable coefficients. Hence he attempted to bring production theory into closer proximity with the concrete facts by developing the apparatus to deal with all these cases. This is all there is to Pareto's so-called "refutation" of the marginal productivity theory. His unfortunate use of the word "erroneous," when referring to Walras' assumption, became an occasion for some controversy in which the participants on both sides seem to have imputed more to Pareto than he had in mind (see footnote 59).[60]

In summary, Pareto, like some of his predecessors and contemporaries, argued that the test of an hypothesis is in the truth of its observable implications. However, he went beyond them in his concept of empirically meaningful hypotheses. Finally, factual "realism" of the assumption will be an important factor in evaluating the hypothesis; the empirical value of an hypothesis increases as the factual "realism" of the assumption increases with successive approximations. These propositions represent his contribution to the "verification problem" in economics.

To go into the details of the modern developments regarding the problem of verification would be beyond the scope of this study. Also, the problem is far from settled. In general, with respect to "fundamental" assumptions, Machlup sides with Friedman. That is to say, both claim, for different reasons, that the "reality" of the assumption is not a matter of concern: the "test" of an hypothesis is in the

---

60. It is well known that Pareto and Walras developed a deep-seated mutual dislike for each other. Pareto's use of the word "erroneous" probably stems more from personal reasons than scientific reasons. Cf. Tommaso Giacalone-Monaco, *Pareto-Walras da un carteggio inedito (1891-1901)* (Padova: Cedam, 1957), for a discussion of the personalities.

truth of its observable implications. Melitz, to a great extent, supports the Hutchison position that where a satisfactory test, in terms of predictability, is lacking, the "reality" of the assumption is important. Finally, Samuelson argues that in *all* cases the "reality" of the assumption is important. I have shown that Pareto took a position similar to that of Samuelson. This fact has always remained implicit in the technical discussions of Pareto's contributions to economics.

VII *Conclusion*

I shall now undertake an evaluation of Pareto's place in the development of economic science. In particular, I shall focus attention on Pareto's contribution in relation to modern methodological positions. The choice of modern methodological positions as a criterion for evaluating the significance of Pareto's methodology presents some difficulties, since many of the issues discussed in this study are far from resolved. Nevertheless, there are prevailing views, and these will be presented in this chapter.

The problem of ethical neutrality serves as a good example of an issue that is far from resolved. At first glance, a casual inspection of the literature on the subject would seem to indicate that modern scientific opinion ranges (as it did in Pareto's time) from the view that economics cannot be anything but an ethical discipline to the view that "positive" economics is independent of any ethical position or normative judgments. For instance, T. W. Hutchison has recently argued that Joan Robinson, G. Myrdal, and A. Smithies hold the former opinion, while G. Haberler, M. Friedman, G. Stigler, and L. Robbins are of the latter opinion.[1] He further states that the point of view which claims that "positive" economics is independent of any ethical or normative judgments is the "orthodox" view.[2] Also, he takes the stance that the possible separation of (value-free) "positive" economics and "normative" economics "was almost a basic tenet of the 'orthodox' methodology of economics for about a hundred years from Nassau Senior and J. S. Mill, through Cairnes, J. N. Keynes, Pareto and Max Weber, down to Robbins and Friedman."[3] Finally

1. T. W. Hutchison, *'Positive' Economics and Policy Objectives* (Cambridge, Mass.: Harvard University Press, 1964), pp. 13-14, 48n.
2. *Ibid.,* p. 14.
3. *Ibid.,* p. 18 Hutchison then qualifies this rather sweeping statement by adding that the "orthodox" view "never acquired the exclusive acceptance and dominance of a completely orthodox dogma" *(Ibid.).*

126

he tells us that there has been a recent "wave of criticism and scepticism" regarding the "orthodox" view.[4] Specifically, this "recent scepticism" is said to doubt that value judgments can be completely eliminated from "positive" economics.[5]

Hutchison is incorrect in several respects. Firstly, I have indicated (Chapter III) that both Pareto and Weber came to realize that a "positive" economics devoid of ethical content was not possible, and that all one could hope for was the subjective minimization of value judgments. Hence, Pareto and Weber do not belong to Hutchison's group of "orthodox" methodologists. Furthermore, and what is perhaps more important for judging the significance of Pareto, the overwhelming modern point of view is what Hutchison calls the "recent scepticism," namely, the idea of the subjective minimization of ethical judgments, which derives from Pareto and Weber. I shall deal with the modern view shortly. First I must clear up a source of confusion regarding the problem of ethical neutrality, which has led not only Hutchison astray, but which continues to persist in the literature on the problem. This confusion stems from the failure to distinguish between what I shall call *methodological* judgments and *normative* judgments. In order to make the distinction clear, I shall take the case of Friedman, whom Hutchison calls an "orthodox" methodologist.

To support his claim that Friedman is an "orthodox" methodologist, Hutchison quotes from Friedman: "Positive economics is in principle independent of any particular ethical position or normative judgements."[6] And yet Friedman admits that value judgments are involved in the choice of criteria for judging the validity of a theory, the selection and interpretation of data, the adherence to the canons of formal logic, etc.[7] Then what Friedman seems to be saying (although he is never clear, as is the case with most modern writers) is that some value judgments are a necessary part of all positive science, while others can be dispensed with.

Here again, the vagueness of the terms "value" and "ethical" leads

4. *Ibid.*, pp. 44-45.

5. Apparently, modesty prevents Hutchison from apprising the reader of what his position on the issue is, although he has obviously aligned himself with the "recent sceptics." This is a far cry from the Hutchison of the 1930's, whose positivism was peculiarly similar to Comte's anti-theoretical positivism, rather than to Pareto's, as he claimed. (See Chapter III above.) We shall see in the text above that Hutchison (as well as Robbins) never really has understood Pareto's and Weber's methodology.

6. *Ibid.*, p. 14. Reference is to Milton Friedman, "The Methodology of Positive Economics," in *Essays in Positive Economics* (Chicago: University of Chicago Press, 1953), pp. 3-4.

7. Friedman, *Essays*, pp. 7-16.

to continuous confusion, as it did in Pareto's time. In order to clarify the issue, I shall classify value judgments in terms of the various planes of scientific discourse:

I Methodological judgments: (a) the choice of principles to be followed, i.e., Pareto's "logico-experimental" principles of science imply a value judgment; (b) the scope of study; (c) the choice of methods; (d) criteria for accepting or rejecting theories; (e) professional norms, i.e., efficient allocation of resources, etc.; (f) theoretical assumptions, etc.[8]

II Normative judgments: (a) personal ethics of the observer regarding what is best for society; (b) normative principles (Walras' advocacy of perfect competition, or the utilitarians' rationalism, etc.); (c) policy judgments.

The crucial difference between the two types of judgments is this: judgments involved in positive economics are *methodological,* pertaining to the philosophy of science, and mainly concerned with investigations into the nature of society (what is), whereas judgments in normative economics are concerned with what is best for society (what ought to be) in accordance with the observer's ethics.

Both Pareto and Weber spoke of the subjective minimization of ethical judgments. What they had in mind was the elimination of *normative* judgments from economic *science,* at the same time fully realizing that methodological judgments were a necessary part of positive science.[9] And it is precisely here that the significance of their contribution to the issue of ethical neutrality is to be found. For Pareto and Weber were the precursors of the modern view (often implicit) that positive science aims at eliminating *normative* judgments, not *methodological* judgments. This position is suggested in the works of Friedman, Samuelson, I. M. D. Little, Myrdal, Smithies, Morgenstern, Stigler, and Haberler, to mention a few.[10] Of course, I do not

8. The reader can probably think of more examples. Nevertheless, these will suffice to show what I have in mind when I speak of methodological judgments.

9. As regards Weber, this fact is not understood even today. Leo Strauss, *Natural Right and History* (Chicago: University of Chicago Press, 1953), pp. 35-80, completely misses the point when he insists that Weber argued for a completely value-free social science. Weber was referring to what I have called *normative* judgments!

10. Cf. Friedman, *Essays,* pp. 1-16; Paul A. Samuelson, *Foundations of Economic Analysis* (Cambridge, Mass.: Harvard, 1947), pp. 219-20, 250; I. M. D. Little, *A Critique of Welfare Economics* (London: Clarendon, 1950), chap. v; G. Myrdal, *The Political Element in Economic Theory,* trans. P. Streeten (London: Routledge, 1953), p. vii; A. Smithies, *Economics and Public Policy* (Washington, D. C.: Brookings Lectures, 1954, 1955), p. 2; O.

intend to convey the impression that all these authors are unanimous in their interpretation of the degree to which normative judgments actually occur in economic science. I simply point out that the conception of a clearcut distinction between positive and normative economics, *with positive economics being value-free* (free from methodological judgments, also), is held by few economists today.[11] The idea of a value-free science has also been rejected by writers in other social sciences, as well as in the philosophy of science.[12]

We recall that Pareto's views on positive economics also applied to positive policy. That is to say, Pareto believed that if the "real" norms obtaining in a society could be identified, then questions of policy would have a positive basis, since they would reflect the community's norms rather than the subjective norms of the individual observer. Under such circumstances, policy would be in the purview of positive science in the same sense that "welfare" economics is a part of positive economics.[13] Perhaps Friedman is overly op-

Morgenstern, *On the Accuracy of Economic Observations* (Princeton: Princeton University Press, 1963), p. 127; G. Stigler, *Production and Distribution Theories* (New York: Macmillan, 1946), p. 385, suggests that the selection of theoretical assumptions implies some degree of value judgment; G. Haberler, "Review of *Money, Growth, and Methodology and Other Essays,* H. Hegeland, ed.," *American Economic Review,* LIII (March, 1963), 145, seems to complain more about the inclusion of normative judgments rather than of methodological judgments in positive economics.

11. As far I have been able to find, L. Robbins, *An Essay on The Nature and Significance of Economic Science* (London: Macmillan, 1932), has not altered his view. Hence, he is the only person mentioned by Hutchison who belongs to what Hutchison has called the "orthodox" (if there ever was such a thing) methodology.

12. I shall only refer to some of these writers, since I wish the discussion to remain in an economics context. Cf. K. R. Popper, *The Open Society and Its Enemies* (Princeton, N. J.: Princeton University Press, 1950), p. 369 n.; L. Strauss, *Natural Right,* pp. 35-80; Paul H. Furfey, *The Scope and Method of Sociology* (New York: Harper, 1953), chap. iv; J. A. Passmore, "Can the Social Sciences be Value-Free?" *Proceedings of the Tenth International Congress of Philosophy,* II, (1949), 1024-26; Howard Becker, *Through Values to Social Interpretation* (Durham, N. C.: Duke University Press, 1950); F. Kaufmann, *Methodology of the Social Sciences* (New York: Humanities, 1964), chaps. ix, xv; W. H. Werkmeister, "Social Science and the Problem of Value," *Scientism and Values,* eds. Schoeck and Wiggins (Princeton: Van Nostrand, 1960), pp. 1-21; Everett W. Hall, *Modern Science and Human Values* (Princeton: Van Nostrand, 1956); Wolfgang Köhler, *The Place of Value in a World of Facts* (New York: Liveright, 1938); Bertrand Russell, *The Scientific Outlook* (New York: Norton & Co., 1962).

13. Although welfare economics deals with what ought to be, it does so "objectively," since it does not involve interpersonal comparisons of individual utilities by the observer. Pareto, it will be recalled, carried the same reasoning to his sociological "utility" theory: he believed that the identification of the "real" norms of a society would allow "objective" *social* welfare judgments for policy purposes.

tomistic when he too states that the progress of positive economics will tend to reduce subjective differences in economic policy: ". . . differences about economic policy among disinterested citizens derive predominately from different predictions about the economic consequences of taking action—differences that in principle can be eliminated by the progress of positive economics—rather than fundamental differences in basic values."[14] What is important is that both Pareto and Friedman see the development of positive science bringing policy within the purview of that science, and further eroding the base of normative economics. I have also pointed to the increasing interest in the positive basis for economic policy on the part of others.[15] Although the suggested approaches of various writers differ from that of Pareto, the methodology is very similar. All such viewpoints stem from a desire to strengthen the positive basis for policy, in an area which has been historically normative.

Pareto was the first among economists to call attention to the need for "positive policy." His methodology was reflected in his own researches. He gave to economics an "objective" criterion (Pareto Optimum) for making economic welfare judgments. Later, in his sociology, he attempted to provide another type of "objective" criterion—the "real" norms of society. Hence Pareto's endeavors represented a program aimed at establishing a positive basis for policy.

I turn next to the problem of scope. The idea of a specialized discipline, dealing with specialized actions, and making specialized policy recommendations, was repugnant to the German historical economists, economic-sociologists, social philosophers, most reformers (who were often interested in a wider scope), and others. I have already discussed the methodological basis for the views of the Germans and Comte. I shall not go into them any further, except to say that the only view that possessed any substance was that which recognized the intimate relationship between economic and non-economic phenomena.

In general, those economists who accepted as valid the delimitation of the scope of economics according to a specific class of human action recognized the interdependency of economic and non-economic phenomena. In fact, Marshall widened the scope of his "economics" to a point where it became a kind of applied sociology. Nevertheless, very often they did not go beyond a mere recognition of such interdependencies. That is, they never really worked out the

14. Friedman, *Essays,* pp. 3-4.
15. William D. Grampp, "On the History of Thought and Policy," *American Economic Review,* LV (May, 1965), 128-42.

methodological implications of such a recognition for theory and policy. There have been exceptions in some areas of economics, however, such as fiscal and development theory, which have developed *along Pareto's exhortations* (by widening the scope of their researches to include non-economic aspects).

The important question for the purpose of this chapter is to what extent does the profession, in general, accept Pareto's stance that economists must either expand the scope of their positive researches to include non-economic phenomena, or else must supplement economic theory with the theories of other social science disciplines, which deal with non-economic phenomena? I can answer by saying that an increasing number of outstanding economists are disturbed by the rather restrictive scope of economics, especially for policy purposes. For instance, J. R. Hicks precisely expresses Pareto's objections to the concept of strictly "economic" welfare. Hicks maintains that the economist has been allowed and even encouraged to hold that if he:

> . . . has shown that a particular course of action is to be recommended, *for economic reasons,* he has done his job. I would now say that if he limits his function in that manner, he does not rise to his responsibilities. It is impossible to make "economic" proposals that do not have "non-economic" aspects, as the Welfarist would call them; when the economist makes a recommendation, he is responsible for it in the round; all aspects of the recommendation, whether he chooses to label them economic or not, are his concern.[16]

Concern for the multidimensional (socio-economic) nature of goals and the resulting implications for policy has also been expressed recently by J. Viner:

> Those of us who are economic theorists are only too familiar with models which assume a single goal, treated as if it were endowed with a single characteristic varying only in quantity or degree, such as "economic welfare." . . . Such models are indeed the major part of our professional inventory. The legislator, on the other hand, is, or should be, always conscious that he is repeatedly facing the necessity of choosing between extensive combinations of objectives, all of which clamour for consideration.[17]

In Paretian terms, the problem of proper "policy mix" calls attention to the need for social goals considerations, consisting of both economic and non-economic objectives.

16. John R. Hicks, *Essays in World Economics* (Oxford: Clarendon Press, 1959), pp. viii-xi.
17. Jacob Viner, *International Trade and Economic Development* (Oxford: Clarendon Press, 1953), p. 2.

T. Koopmans and J. Marschak express sentiments similar to those of Hicks and Viner, although they use a somewhat different approach. Marschak tells us that:

For the economy as a whole, endogenous variables can be roughly identified with what are often called "economic variables." These are usually the quantities (stocks or flows) and prices of goods and services, or their aggregates and averages, such as national income, total investment, price level, wage level, and so on. The exogenous variables and the structural parameters are, roughly, "noneconomic variables" (also called "data" in the economic literature) and may include the weather and technological, psychological, and sociological conditions as well as legal rules and political decisions. But the boundary is movable. Should political science ever succeed in explaining political situations (and hence legislation itself) by economic causes, institutional variables . . . would have to be counted as endogenous.[18]

In the last sentence of the above citation, Marschak is anticipating a development which would integrate economic and non-economic (in this case political) theories, in precise concurrence with Pareto's methodology.

Finally, K. Boulding expresses doubts as to the efficacy of "applied economics" in dealing with concrete problems. Here again reference is made to the broader social environment in order to deal with such problems: "I have been gradually coming under the conviction, disturbing for a professional theorist, that there is no such thing as economics—there is only social science applied to economic problems."[19] Boulding is expressing the same concern that Pareto did when, on the occasion of his jubilee at Lausanne, he admitted that very often the conclusions of economic theory were not verified by "experience." We recall that he set out to overcome this difficulty by supplementing economic theory with sociological theory.

Notice that the concern for the mutual dependence of economic and non-economic phenomena, with its implications for scope and policy, is being expressed by *theorists,* who have acquired an impressive stature in the economics profession. Their observations are not those of antitheoretical economists, as was the case with Pareto's contemporaries. In other words, the above writers are following a

18. Jacob Marschak, "Measurements for Policy and Prediction," in *Studies in Econometric Method,* eds. Hood and Koopmans (New York: John Wiley, 1950), p. 10. For similar views by T. Koopmans see: "When Is an Equation System Complete for Statistical Purposes?," *Statistical Inference in Dynamic Economic Models,* Cowles Commission Monograph 10, ed. T. C. Koopmans (New York: John Wiley, 1950), pp. 393-409.

19. Kenneth Boulding, *A Reconstruction of Economics* (New York: John Wiley, 1950), p. vii.

line of thought that stems from Pareto. For Pareto did not propose abandoning economic theory, he merely suggested expanding the scope of economic theory to include non-economic phenomena in order to render a better approximation to concrete reality. Hence, although he defended specialized analytical researches, he called attention to their limitations when dealing with concrete problems.

I have mentioned W. Arthur Lewis' observation that during the second quarter of the twentieth century, the implications of the explicit recognition of the mutual dependence of economic and non-economic phenomena were stated not to be the proper business of economists. This view is changing today, as exemplified by the thoughts of Hicks, Viner, Marschak, and Boulding. These writers have taken a methodological position very similar to that of Pareto, although their particular approaches in dealing with the problem of scope may vary. Here is another instance of the lasting contribution of Pareto's methodology.

We have seen that another of the great contemporary methodological issues of the nineteenth century involved the validity of generalizing concepts in the social sciences. At bottom, the issue was whether the subject matter of the social sciences was such that they required methods quite distinct from physical science methods. The battle surrounding this issue was waged on methodological grounds, as I have shown. Pareto took the methodological position that there was no formal basis for the distinction between the physical and social sciences. Hence, for him, the methods of the physical sciences were a valid source of scientific knowledge. He even demonstrated the efficacy of physical science methods in his own researches, especially by his pioneering achievement in what has become known as econometrics. Recall, though, that even the outstanding methodologist, J. N. Keynes, argued against the numerical determination of functions.

The development of economics has shown an almost overwhelming tendency to follow Pareto's methodological lines.[20] That is to say,

---

20. This also seems to be the case in the philosophy of science. I shall merely refer to some important publications in this area, since I wish to confine the textual discussion to economics proper. Cf. Ernest Nagel, "Problems of Concepts and Theory Formation in the Social Sciences," *Science, Language, and Human Rights* (American Philosophical Association, Eastern Division, Philadelphia: University of Pennsylvania Press, 1952), pp. 43-64; C. G. Hempel, *Ibid.*, pp. 65-86; Alfred Schutz, "Concept and Theory Formation in the Social Sciences," *The Journal of Philosophy,* LI (April, 1954), 257-73. For a suggested compromise between the "phenomenological" and "naturalistic" viewpoints, see: Leon J. Goldstein, "The Phenomenological and Naturalistic Approaches to the Social," *Methodos,* XIII (1961), 225-38. For a criticism of the "naturalist" viewpoint, see: Thelma Lavine, "Note to

mathematized theory and econometric researches have gained wide acceptance in modern economics. These methods place reliance upon *analytical* generalizations. What is important for the purposes of this chapter is that implicit in the widespread use of such methods is the recognition that no formal distinction exists between the physical and social science methods, a position taken by Pareto. The fact that this is the prevailing opinion among economists is so obvious that it hardly needs justifying.[21]

Nevertheless, there are critics of the prevailing view today, as there were in Pareto's time. And for the most part, the methodological basis for attacking this view is often very similar to the old arguments raised by Pareto's contemporaries. Take for example Von Mises, who has been an outspoken critic of modern economic methodology.

Von Mises distinguishes between epistemology, which "deals with the mental phenomena of human life, with man as he thinks and acts," and "logical positivism," more properly applicable to the physical sciences.[22] His science of human action has as one of its branches "praxeology," which is based on *a priori* "self-evident" propositions, "fully, clearly and necessarily present in every human mind."[23] Because of the alleged duality of mind and matter, he proposes that economics abandon its "logical positivism," together with its corresponding methods, and adopt "praxeology."

The way in which the philosophy of logical positivism depicts the universe is defective. It comprehends only what can be recognized by the experimental methods of the natural sciences. It ignores the human mind as well as human action.

. . . .

As far as the empiricist principle of logical positivism refers to experi-

---

Naturalists on the Human Spirit," *Journal of Philosophy*, L (Feb., 1953), 145-54. Finally, for a more moderate position than Lavine's, see: Maurice Natanson, "A Study in Philosophy and the Social Sciences," *Social Research*, XXV (Summer, 1958), 158-72.

21. Instead, I shall refer the reader to Sidney Schoeffler, *The Failures of Economics: A Diagnostic Study* (Cambridge, Mass.: Harvard University Press, 1955). Although Schoeffler is critical of economists for proceeding "on their endeavors as if economics were a science like physics or psychology," his book does serve to show that the prevailing methodological position recognizes no formal distinction between physical and social science methods. In fact, he devotes the major part of his work (chaps. iii-vii) to a critique of models and methods developed as a consequence of the prevailing methodological position.

22. Ludwig Von Mises, *The Ultimate Foundation of Economic Science* (Princeton: Van Nostrand, 1963), pp. 2-3.

23. *Ibid.*, p. 5.

mental methods of the natural sciences, it merely asserts what is not questioned by anybody. As far as it rejects the epistemological principles of the sciences of human action, it is not only entirely wrong. It is also knowingly and intentionally undermining the intellectual foundations of Western civilization.[24]

I have devoted some space to Von Mises to show an interesting aspect of methodology: old views are often rejected only to be reared under new names. Von Mises' "praxeology" has not been popular among economists, for the same reason that they have ignored the exhortations of the German advocates of "intuition." That is, his "praxeology" rests on the assumption that "self-evident" propositions are a valid source of scientific knowledge. Both advocates of "praxeology" and "intuition" have ignored a fundamental problem of science: the manner by which subjective experience is to be "objectified," or, put in other terms, the criterion for accepting or rejecting theories. What is self-evident or intuitively obvious to one observer may not be so to someone else. How, then, are differing subjective experiences to be reconciled? "Logical positivism" (to use Von Mises' expression) has chosen verifiability as a criterion, and the problem has become known as the verification problem. But the critics of "logical positivism" have tended to ignore this important problem, for as Pareto has pointed out, faith by its very nature is exclusive: if one feels possessed with "truth" there is little room remaining for skepticism or doubt.[25]

On the other hand, one of the greatest concerns of modern economic methodologists has been precisely with finding an "objective" criterion for accepting or rejecting hypotheses—the verification problem. Modern economics is not concerned with the psychological or social origins of a scientific argument; as Pareto and Weber pointed out, such considerations are superfluous for science. Today, the main concern is, as it was for Pareto, the "objective" aspect of a proposition—"not by the manner in which it has been conceived, but by the verification that can be made of it."[26]

In general, the economics profession has accepted the principle of

24. *Ibid.*, pp. 125, 133.
25. It is perhaps less than an accident that the most virulent attacks upon scientific methodology have come from reformers, who have had little else in common. For instance, some of the German historians (the "socialists of the chair," as Schumpeter calls them), attacked the "scientific ethic" of the English, French, and Italians, whereas Von Mises believes that scientific methodology ("logical positivism") is "sapping the foundations of Western civilization," and contributing to the development of communism, socialism, and fascism (*Ibid.*, pp. 128-33). Strange bedfellows indeed!
26. See Chapter V above.

prediction as a criterion for testing theories.[27] This criterion stems from J. S. Mill, J. N. Keynes, and Pareto. I have shown that Samuelson's "operationally meaningful theorems" concept also stems from Pareto, who spoke of empirically meaningful hypotheses. The Pareto-Samuelson "empirically meaningful hypotheses" concept also enjoys current popularity among economists, especially those interested in the statistical testing of hypotheses.

What controversy does exist with respect to the verification problem centers around the significance of the factual "realism" of assumptions. We recall that Samuelson supports Pareto's position that the practical value of an hypothesis increases as the factual realism of its assumption (assumptions) increases (increase), in *all* cases. The Hutchison-Melitz view considers "realism" to be of significance where a predictive test is lacking. With the exception of Friedman and Machlup, most writers place importance on the "realism" of assumptions, at least in varying degrees. The economics profession has, to a remarkable extent, adopted Pareto's views on the verification problem, although his contribution has always remained implicit in the technical discussions of his contributions to economics.

In summary, modern methodological positions on the issues of ethical neutrality, the scope of economics and sociology, the methodology and method of the social sciences, and the methodology and method of economics closely correspond to Pareto's methodology. Herein lies the lasting contribution of this great methodologist. Pareto's methodological approach to economics in the last quarter of the nineteenth century has become the "orthodox" methodology of modern twentieth-century economics. He was a leader among the precursors of modern economic methodology.

27. See Chapter VI, n. 44 above for the specific writers on the verification problem.

Bibliography

Books

ALLEN, R. G. D. *Mathematical Analysis for Economists*. London: Macmillan & Co., 1938.

ARROW, K. *Social Choice and Individual Values*. New York: John Wiley & Sons, 1951.

BAGEHOT, WILLIAM. *Economic Studies*. London: Longmans, 1888.

BECKER, HOWARD. *Through Values to Social Interpretation*. Durham, N. C.: Duke University Press, 1950.

BENDIX, REINHARD. *Max Weber: An Intellectual Portrait*. Garden City, N. Y.: Doubleday, 1960.

BENTHAM, JEREMY. *An Introduction to the Principles of Morals and Legislation*. 1st edition, 1789. Oxford: Clarendon Press, 1907.

BLAUG, M. *Economic Theory in Retrospect*. Homewood, Ill.: Irwin, 1962.

BORKENAU, FRANZ. *Pareto*. London: Chapman and Hall, 1936.

BOSQUET, G. H. *Vilfredo Pareto, sa vie et son oeuvre*. Paris: Payot et Cie., 1928.

BOULDING, KENNETH. *A Reconstruction of Economics*. New York: John Wiley, 1950.

BOWEN, HOWARD R. *Toward Social Economy*. New York: Rinehart, 1948.

BRIEFS, HENRY. *Three Views of Method in Economics*. Washington, D. C.: Georgetown University Press, 1960.

BUCKLE, HENRY T. *History of Civilization in England*. 3 vols. London: Parker & Son, 1901.

CAIRNES, JOHN E. *Character and Logical Method of Political Economy*. London: Macmillan, 1875.

138 / *Bibliography*

CAPPA, ALBERTO. *Vilfredo Pareto.* Torino: Gobetti, 1924.
CASSIRER, ERNST. *The Problem of Knowledge.* New York: Yale University Press, 1950.
CHARLESWORTH, JAMES C. (ed.). *Mathematics and the Social Sciences, The Utility and Inutility of Mathematics in the Study of Economics, Political Science and Sociology,* A. Symposium. Sponsored by The American Academy of Political and Social Science. Philadelphia: June 1963.
COMTE, AUGUSTE. *Cours de philosophie positive.* 6 vols. Paris: Schleicher, 1830.
DAHL, R. A., AND LINDBLOM, C. E. *Politics, Economics and Welfare.* New York: Harper & Brothers, 1953.
DURKEIM, EMILE. *The Rules of Sociological Method.* Glencoe, Ill.: Free Press, 1938.
EDGEWORTH, FRANCIS Y. *Mathematical Psychics.* London: Kegan Paul & Co., 1882.
EISERMANN, G. *Vilfredo Pareto als Nationalökonom und Soziologe.* Tübingen: Mohr, 1961.
EWING, A. C. (ed.). *The Idealistic Tradition.* Glencoe, Ill.: The Free Press, 1957.
FURFEY, PAUL. *The Scope and Method of Sociology.* New York: Harper, 1953.
GIACALONE-MONACO, TOMMASO. *Pareto-Walras da un carteggio inedito (1891-1901).* Padova: Cedam, 1957.
GIDE AND RIST. *A History of Economic Doctrines.* Translated by R. Richards. 2nd ed. Boston: D. C. Heath & Co., 1948.
GOSSEN, H. H. *Entwickelung der Gesetze des menschlichen Verkehrs.* Berlin: R. L. Prager, 1927.
HALL, EVERETT W. *Modern Science and Human Values.* Princeton: Van Nostrand, 1956.
HEGEL, GEORG WILHELM FRIEDRICH. *Die Naturphilosophie.* Part II of the *System der Philosophie* and Vol. IX (1929) of *Sämtliche Werke,* 20 vols. Stuttgart: F. Frommann, 1927-30.
HEIMANN, EDWARD. *History of Economic Doctrines.* New York: Oxford, 1964.
HICKS, JOHN R. *Value and Capital.* Oxford: Clarendon Press, 1939.
———. *Essays in World Economics.* Oxford: Clarendon Press, 1959.
HOOK, SIDNEY. *From Hegel to Marx.* London: Gollancy, 1936.
HUTCHISON, T. W. *The Significance and Basic Postulates of Economic Theory.* London: Macmillan, 1938.
———. *A Review of Economic Doctrines 1870-1929.* Oxford: Clarendon Press, 1953.
———. *'Positive' Economics and Policy Objectives.* Cambridge, Mass.: Harvard University Press, 1964.
JOHNSTON, J. *Econometric Methods.* New York: McGraw-Hill, 1960.

KAUFMANN, FELIX. *Methodology of the Social Sciences.* New York: Humanities, 1964.

KEYNES, JOHN NEVILLE. *The Scope and Method of Political Economy.* 4th ed., 1917. New York: A. M. Kelly, 1963. (First published in 1890.)

KLEIN, LAWRENCE. *An Introduction to Econometrics.* Englewood Cliffs, New Jersey: Prentice-Hall, 1962.

KÖHLER, WOLFGANG. *The Place of Value in a World of Facts.* New York: Liveright, 1938.

LANGE, O. AND F. M. TAYLOR. *On the Economic Theory of Socialism.* Minneapolis, Minn.: University of Minnesota Press, 1938.

LEWIS, G. H. *Comte's Philosophy of the Sciences.* London: George Bell and Sons, 1904.

LEWIS, W. ARTHUR. *The Theory of Economic Growth.* Homewood, Ill.: Irwin, 1955.

LINDAHL, ERIK. *Die Gerechtigkeit der Besteurung.* Lund: Gleerupska, 1919. Excerpts translated into English and repinted as: "Some Controversial Questions in the Theory of Taxation," *Classics in the Theory of Public Finance,* ed. Musgrave and Peacock. New York: Macmillan, 1962, pp. 214-32.

LITTLE, I. M. D. *A Critique of Welfare Economics.* London: Clarendon, 1950.

MANNHEIM, KARL. *Essays on the Sociology of Knowledge,* ed. Paul Kecskemeti. New York: Oxford University Press, 1952.

———. *Essays on Sociology and Social Psychology.* New York: Oxford University Press, 1953.

MAQUET, JACQUES. *The Sociology of Knowledge.* Boston: Beacon Press, 1951.

MARSHALL, ALFRED. *Principles of Economics.* 8th ed. London: Macmillan & Co., 1925. (First published in 1890.)

MARX, KARL. *Manifesto of the Communist Party.* Chicago: Kerr, 1888.

———. *A Contribution to the Critique of Political Economy.* Translated by N. I. Stone. New York: International Library Publishing Co., 1904.

MILL, J. S. *Essays on Some Unsettled Questions of Political Economy.* London: J. W. Parker, 1844.

———. *A System of Logic.* London: Longmans, Green & Co., 1884.

———. *Utilitarianism.* London: Longmans, Green, Renle, & Dyer, 1867.

MORGENSTERN, OSKAR. *On the Accuracy of Economic Observations.* Princeton: Princeton University Press, 1963.

MYRDAL, GUNNAR. *The Political Element in Economic Theory.* Translated by P. Streetin. London: Routledge, 1953.

NATANSON, MAURICE (ed.). *Philosophy of the Social Sciences: A Reader.* New York: Random House, 1963.

PANTALEONI, MAFFEO. *Pure Economics.* New York: Kelly and Millman, 1957. Originally published in Italian as *Elementi di economia pura,* and translated into English in 1898.

PARETO, VILFREDO. *Cours d'économie politique.* 2 vols. Lausanne: Librairie de l'Université, 1897.

————. *Les systèmes socialistes.* 2 vols. Paris: Giard et Brière 1902-3.

————. *Manuale d'economia politica.* Milano: Società editrice libraria, 1906. French translation and revision: *Manuel d'économie politique.* Paris: Giard et Brière, 1909.

————. *Trattato di sociologia generale.* 4 vols. Firenze: Barbera, 1916. Translated into English as: *The Mind and Society.* Translated and edited by Arthur Livingston. 4 vols. New York: Harcourt, Brace & Co., 1935.

————. *Jubilé du professor V. Pareto.* Lausanne: Lausanne University, 1920.

————. *Scritti teorici,* Racotti da Giovanni Demaria. Milano: Rodolfo Malfasi Editone, 1953.

————. *Lettere a Maffeo Pantaleoni 1890-1923.* A cura di Gabriele De Rosa. 3 vols. Roma: Edizioni di Storia e Litteratura, 1962.

PARSONS, TALCOTT. *The Structure of Social Action.* York, Pa.: McGraw-Hill, 1937.

PIGOU, ARTHUR. *The Economics of Welfare.* London: Macmillan, 1920.

POPPER, KARL. *The Open Society and Its Enemies.* Princeton, N. J.: Princeton University Press, 1950.

QUESNAY, FRANÇOIS. *Tableau économique.* Paris: Institut national d'études démographiques, 1958.

RICKERT, HEINRICH. *Uber die Grenzen der naturwissenschaftlichen Begriffsbildung.* 1st ed., 1902; 2nd ed., 1913. Tübingen: Mohr, 1929.

————. *Kulturwissenschaft und Naturwissenschaft: ein Vortrag.* Tübingen: Mohr, 1926.

ROBBINS, LIONEL. *An Essay on the Nature and Significance of Economic Science.* London: Macmillan, 1932.

ROBINSON, JOAN. *Economic Philosophy.* Chicago: Aldine, 1962.

ROLL, ERIC. *A History of Economic Thought.* Englewood Cliffs, N. J.: Prentice-Hall, 1939.

RUSSELL, BERTRAND. *The Scientific Outlook.* New York: Norton & Co., 1962.

SAMUELSON, PAUL A. *Foundations of Economic Analysis.* Cambridge, Mass.: Harvard, 1947.

————. *Economics: An Introductory Analysis.* 6th ed. New York: McGraw-Hill, 1956.

SCHOEFFLER, SIDNEY. *The Failures of Economics: A Diagnostic Study.* Cambridge, Mass.: Harvard University Press, 1955.

SCHUMPETER, JOSEPH. *Economic Doctrine and Method.* Translated by R. Aris. London: George Allen and Unwin, 1954.
————. *History of Economic Analysis.* New York: Oxford University Press, 1954.
SMITH, ADAM. *An Inquiry into the Nature and Causes of the Wealth of Nations.* London: A. Strahan and T. Cadell, 1793.
————. *The Theory of Moral Sentiments.* 2 vols. "Last English edition." Boston: Wells and Lilly, 1827.
SMITHIES, A. *Economics and Public Policy.* Washington, D. C.: Brookings Lectures, 1954, 1955.
SOREL, GEORGES. *Réflexions sur la violence.* Paris: Riviere, 1908.
SPENCER, HERBERT. *The Classification of the Sciences.* New York: Appleton, 1864.
————. *Principles of Sociology.* New York: Appleton, 1896.
STARK, WERNER. *The Sociology of Knowledge.* Glencoe, Ill.: The Free Press, 1958.
————. *The Fundamental Forms of Social Thought.* London: Routledge & Kegan Paul, 1962.
STIGLER, GEORGE. *Production and Distribution Theories.* New York: Macmillan, 1946.
STRAUSS, LEO. *Natural Right and History.* Chicago: University of Chicago Press, 1953.
VINER, JACOB. *International Trade and Economic Development.* Oxford: Clarendon Press, 1953.
VON MISES, LUDWIG. *Epistemological Problems of Economics.* Princeton: Van Nostrand, 1960.
————. *The Ultimate Foundation of Economic Science.* Princeton: Van Nostrand, 1962.
VON SCHELTING, ALEXANDER. *Max Weber's Wissenschaftslehre.* Tübingen: Mohr, 1934.
WALRAS, LÉON. *Eléments d'économie politique pure.* 4th (definitive) ed. Paris: Pichon et Durand-Auzias, 1926. (First published in 1874.)
————. *Correspondence of Léon Walras and Related Papers,* ed. William Jaffe. 3 vols. Amsterdam: North Holland, 1965.
WATSON, JOHN. *Comte, Mill and Spencer.* Glasgow: James Maclehose and Sons, 1895.
WEBER, MAX. *Wirtschaft und Gesellschaft.* Originally printed as the third part of *Grundriss der Sozialökonomik.* 2 vols. Tübingen: Mohr, 1913. Reprinted in *Gesammelte Aufsätze zur Wissenschaftslehre.* Tübingen: Mohr, 1922.
————. *The Protestant Ethic and the Spirit of Capitalism.* Translated by Talcott Parsons. London: George Allen & Unwin, 1930.
————. *From Max Weber: Essays in Sociology.* Translated, edited, and introduced by H. H. Gerth and C. Wright Mills. New York: Oxford, 1946.

————. *The Theory of Social and Economic Organization*. Translated by A. M. Henderson and Talcott Parsons. Ed. T. Parsons. Glencoe, Ill.: The Free Press, 1947.

————. *The Methodology of the Social Sciences*. Translated and edited by E. Shils and H. Finch. Glencoe, Ill.: The Free Press, 1949.

WICKSELL, KNUT. *Finanztheoretische Untersuchungen*. Jena: 1896. Excerpts translated into English and reprinted as: "A New Principle of Just Taxation." *Classics in the Theory of Public Finance*. Ed. Richard A. Musgrave and Alan T. Peacock. New York: Macmillan, 1962, pp. 72-118.

WICKSTEED, PHILIP. *Common Sense of Political Economy*. London: Routledge, Kegan Paul, 1933.

WOLD, HERMAN. *Demand Analysis: A Study in Econometrics*. New York: Wiley, 1953.

Articles

AMOROSO, LUIGI. "Vilfredo Pareto," *Econometrica,* VI (Jan., 1938), 1-21.

BARONE, ENRICO. "Il Ministro della produzione nello stato colletivista," *Giornale degli economisti,* XXXVII (Sept., 1908), 267-93; (Oct., 1908), 391-414.

BERGSON, ABRAM. "A Reformulation of Certain Aspects of Welfare Economics," *Quarterly Journal of Economics,* LII (Feb., 1938), 310-34.

————. "Socialist Economics," in *Survey of Contemporary Economics*. Ed. H. S. Ellis. Homewood, Ill.: Irwin, 1948, pp. 412-48.

BLACK, DUNCAN. "On the Rationale of Group Decision-Making," *Journal of Political Economy,* LVI (Feb., 1948), 23-24.

————. "The Decision of a Committee Using a Special Majority," *Econometrica,* XVI (July, 1948), 245-61.

————. "Wicksell's Principle in the Distribution of Taxation," in *Economic Essays in Commemoration of the Dundee School of Economics*. Ed. J. K. Eastman. London: Culross & Sons, 1955, pp. 7-23.

BOBBIO, NORBERTO. "Introduction to Pareto's Sociology," *Banca Nazional del Lavoro, Quarterly Review,* No. 69 (June, 1964), pp. 183-206.

BORGATTA, GINO. "I rapporti fra la scienza economica e la sociologia nell'opera Paretiana," *Giornale degli economisti,* LXIV (Jan.-Feb., 1924).

BUCHANAN, JAMES M. "The Pure Theory of Government Finance: A Suggested Approach," *Journal of Political Economy,* LVII (Dec., 1949), 496-505.

————. "Social Choice, Democracy and Free Markets," *Journal of Political Economy,* LXII (Apr., 1954), 114-23.

BUSINO, G. "Pareto e le authorità di Losanna," *Giornale degli economisti,* N. S. XXII (March-April, 1963), 260-303.

CANNAN, EDWIN. "Editor's Introduction," in Adam Smith, *The Wealth of Nations.* New York: Modern Library, 1937.

FRIEDMAN, MILTON. "The Methodology of Positive Economics," in *Essays in Positive Economics.* Chicago: University of Chicago Press, 1953, pp. 3-43.

GIACALONE-MONACO, TOMMASO. "Le 'Cronache' politiche ed economiche di Pareto," *Giornale degli economisti,* N. S. XIX (Nov.-Dec., 1960), 788-815.

GOLDSTEIN, LEON J. "The Phenomenological and Naturalistic Approaches to the Social," *Methodos,* XIII (1961), 257-73.

GRAMPP, WILLIAM D. "On the History of Thought and Policy," *American Economic Review,* LV (May, 1965), 128-42.

HAAVELMO, T. "Quantitative Research in Agricultural Economics: The Interdependence between Agriculture and the National Economy," *Journal of Farm Economics,* XXIX (Nov., 1947), 910-14.

HABERLER, G. "Review of *Money, Growth, and Methodology and Other Essays,* H. Hegeland, ed.," *American Economic Review,* LIII (March, 1963), 143-47.

HARRINGTON, JOHN. "Vilfredo Pareto," in *Social Theorists.* Ed. C. Mihanovich. Milwaukee: Bruce Publishing Co., 1953.

HICKS, JOHN R. "Marginal Productivity and the Principle of Variation," *Economic Journal,* XII (Feb., 1932), 79-88.

HILDRETH, CLIFFORD. "Alternative Condition of Social Ordering," *Econometrica,* XXI (Jan., 1953), 81-94.

HUTCHISON, T. W. "Professor Machlup on Verification in Economics," *Southern Economic Journal,* XXII (Apr., 1956), 476-83.

JOHNSON, N. O. "The Pareto Law," *The Review of Economic Statistics,* XIX (Jan., 1937), 20-26.

KOOPMANS, T. C. "When Is an Equation System Complete for Statistical Purposes?," in *Statistical Inference in Dynamic Economic Models,* Cowles Commission Monograph 10. Ed. T. C. Koopmans. New York: John Wiley, 1950.

LAVINE, THELMA. "Note to Naturalists on the Human Spirit," *Journal of Philosophy,* L (Feb., 1953), 145-54.

LEONTIEF, WASSILY. "Interrelation of Prices, Output, Savings and Investment," *The Review of Economic Statistics,* XIX (Aug., 1937) 109-32.

LOPREATO, JOSEPH. "A Functionalist Reappraisal of Pareto's Sociology," *American Journal of Sociology,* LXIX (May, 1964), 639-46.

MACHLUP, FRITZ. "The Problem of Verification in Economics," *Southern Economic Journal,* XXII (July, 1955), 1-21.

———. "Rejoinder to a Reluctant Ultra-Empiricist," *Southern Economic Journal,* XXII (Apr., 1956), 483-93.

———. "Operational Concepts and Mental Constructs in Model and Theory Formation," *Giornale degli economisti e annali di economia,* XIX (Sept.-Oct., 1960), 553-82.

———. "Professor Samuelson on Theory and Realism," *American Economic Review,* LIV. (Sept., 1964), 733-36.

MANDELBROT, BENOIT. "New Methods in Statistical Economics," *Journal of Political Economy,* LXXI (Nov., 1963), 421-40.

MARSCHAK, JACOB. "Measurements for Policy and Prediction," in *Studies in Econometric Method.* Ed. Hood and Koopmans. New York: John Wiley, 1950, pp. 1-26.

MELITZ, JACK. "Friedman and Machlup on the Significance of Testing Economic Assumptions," *Journal of Political Economy,* LXXIII (Feb., 1965), 37-60.

MILL, JAMES. "Essay on Government," *Encyclopedia Brittanica* (suppl., 1823).

MILLIKAN, MAX. "Pareto's Sociology," *Econometrica,* IV (Dec., 1936), 324-37.

MORTARA, GIORGIO. "Pareto statistico," *Giornale degli economisti,* LXIV (Jan.-Feb., 1924), 120-25.

NAGEL, ERNEST. "Problems of Concepts and Theory Formation in the Social Sciences," in *Science, Language, and Human Rights.* American Philosophical Association, Eastern Division. Philadelphia: University of Pennsylvania Press, 1952, pp. 43-64.

NATANSON, MAURICE. "A Study in Philosophy and the Social Sciences," *Social Research,* XXV (Summer, 1958), 158-72.

NOVICK, DAVID. "Mathematics: Logic, Quantity and Method," *The Review of Economics and Statistics,* XXXVI (Nov., 1954), 357-58.

PANTALEONI, MAFFEO. "Vilfredo Pareto," *Economic Journal,* XXXIII (Sept., 1923), 582-90.

———. "In occasione della morte di Pareto: reflessioni," *Giornale degli economisti,* LXIV (Jan.-Feb., 1924), 1-19.

PARETO, VILFREDO. "Considerazioni sui principii fondamentali dell'economia politica pura," *Giornale degli economisti,* IV (March, 1892), 389-420; (June, 1892), 485-512; V (Aug., 1892), 119-57; VI (Jan., 1893), 1-37; VII (Oct., 1893), 279-321.

———. "La mortalità infantile e il costo dell'uomo adulto," *Giornale degli economisti,* VII (Nov., 1893), 451-56.

———. "Teoria matematica dei cambi forestieri," *Giornale degli economisti,* VIII (Feb., 1894), 142-73.

———. "Il modo di figuari i fenomeno economici (A proposito di un libro del dottore Fornasari)," *Giornale degli economisti,* XII (Jan., 1896), 75-87.

———. "La curva della entrate e le osservazioni dell professor Edgeworth," *Giornale degli economisti,* XIII (Nov., 1896), 439-48.

———. "Aggiunta allo studio curva della entrate," *Giornale degli economisti,* XIV (Jan., 1897), 15-26.

———. "The New Theories of Economics," *The Journal of Political Economy,* V. (Sept., 1897), 485-502.

———. "Quelques exemples d'application des méthodes d'interpolation à la statistique," *Journal de la Société de statistique de Paris* (Nov., 1897), pp. 367-79.

———. "Tables pour faciliter l'application de la méthode de moindres carrés," *Journal de statistique suisse* (1899), pp. 121-50.

———. "Sul fenomeno economico. Lettera a Benedetto Croce," *Giornale degli economisti,* XXI (Aug., 1900), 139-62.

———. "Sul principio economico," *Giornale degli economisti,* XXII (Feb., 1901), 131-38.

———. "Le nuovo teorie economiche. Appunti," *Giornale degli economisti,* XXIII (Sept., 1901), 235-52.

———. "Di un nuovo errore nello interpretare le teorie dell'economia matematica," *Giornale degli economisti,* XXV (Nov., 1902), 401-33.

———. "L'interpolazione per la ricerca delle leggi economiche," *Giornale degli economisti,* XXXIV (March, 1907), 266-85; XXXVI (June, 1908), 423-53.

———. "Walras," *Economic Journal,* XX (March, 1910), 138-39.

———. "Il massimo di utilità per una collectività in sociologia," *Giornale degli economisti,* XLVI (Apr., 1913), 337-38.

———. "Economia sperimentale," *Giornale degli economisti,* LII (July-Aug., 1918), 1-18.

———. "Economie Mathématique," *Encyclopédie des Sciences Mathématiques,* Tome I, Vol. IV, Fasc. 4. Paris: Teubner, Gauthier, Villars, 1911. Translated into English as: "Mathematical Economics," *International Economic Papers,* V(1955), 58-102.

PASSMORE, J. A. "Can the Social Sciences be Value-Free?" *Proceedings of the Tenth International Congress of Philosophy,* II (1949), 1024-26.

ROYCE, JOSIAH. "Hegel's Phenomenology of Mind," in *Lectures on Modern Idealism.* New Haven: Yale University Press, 1919, pp. 161-212.

SAMUELSON, PAUL A. "International Trade and the Equalization of Factor Prices," *Economic Journal,* LVIII (June, 1948), 163-84.

———. "International Factor-Price Equalization Once Again," *Economic Journal,* LIX (June, 1949), 181-97.

————, et al. "Mathematics in Economics: A Discussion of Mr. Novick's Article," *The Review of Economics and Statistics,* XXXVI (Nov., 1954), 359-86.

————. "Problems of Methodology—Discussion," *American Economic Review, Proceedings,* LIII (May, 1963), 231-36.

————. "Theory and Realism: A Reply," *American Economic Review,* LIV (Sept., 1964), 736-39.

SCHULTZ, HENRY. "Marginal Productivity and the Pricing Process," *Journal of Political Economy,* XXXVII (Oct., 1929), 505-51.

SCHUMPETER, JOSEPH. "Vilfredo Pareto (1848-1923)," *Quarterly Journal of Economics,* LXIII (May, 1949), 147-73.

SCHUTZ, ALFRED. "Concept and Theory Formation in the Social Sciences," *The Journal of Philosophy,* LI (April, 1954), 257-73.

SPENGLER, J. J. "Pareto on Population I," *Quarterly Journal of Economics,* LVIII (Aug., 1944), 593-98.

————. "Pareto on Population II," *Quarterly Journal of Economics,* LIX (Nov., 1944), 107-33.

STARK, WERNER. "In Search of the True Pareto," *British Journal of Sociology,* XIV (June, 1963), 103-12.

WERKMEISTER, W. H. *"Social Science and the Problem of Value,"* in *Scientism and Values.* Ed. Schoeck and Wiggins. Princeton: Van Nostrand, 1960.

WICKSELL, KNUT. "Vilfredo Pareto, *Cours d'économie politique,"* *Zeitschrift für Volkswirtschaft, Sozialpolitik und Verwaltung* (1897), pp. 159-66. Reprinted in English in *Selected Papers of Knut Wicksell.* Ed. Erick Lindahl. Cambridge, Mass.: Harvard, 1958, pp. 141-58.

ZUCCARINI, OLIVIERO. "Politica e sociologia di Vilfredo Pareto," *Comunità,* No. 94 (Nov. 15, 1961), pp. 84-101.

Unpublished Material

MORGENSTERN, OSKAR. "Pareto Optimum and Economic Organization," *Econometric Research Program Research Memorandum No. 63.* Princeton: Unpublished, January 24, 1964.

Index

A

Abstraction, 63
Adam Smith Society, 7, 39n, 40, 67
Allen, R. G. D., 13
Amoroso, Luigi, 6n, 7n, 8n, 10, 12. *See* Lausanne school
Antagonists (the Adversaries), 40
Anti-Corn Laws League, 39n
Anti-Rationalism. *See* German historical school, Marx
Aris, R., 62n, 86n
Aristophanes, 8
Aristotle, 31
Arrow, K., 14n
Atomism. *See* Utilitarianism
Austrian school, 12. *See* Böhm-Bawerk, Menger, Weiser

B

Bacon, Francis, 30
Bagehot, William, 58, 105
Barone, Enrico, 10, 12, 45n, 123n. *See* Lausanne school
Bastiat, Frédéric, 40
Becker, Howard, 129n
Bendix, Reinhard, 63n

Bentham, Jeremy, 15n, 16-17, 28, 79n. *See* Utilitarianism
Bergson, Abram, 83n
Black, Duncan, 14n
Blaug, M., 12n, 48n, 123n
Blue Laws, 52n
Bobbio, Norberto, 13n, 31, 35n
Böhm-Bawerk, 12. *See* Austrian school, Literary economists
Borgatta, Gino, 12, 67n. *See* Lausanne school
Borkenau, Franz, 74n
Bosquet, G. H., 6n, 11
Boulding, Kenneth, 132-33
Bowen, Howard R., 14n
Briefs, Henry, 109n
Buchanan, James M., 14n
Buckle, Henry T., 24
Busino, G., 9n

C

Cairnes, John E., 113, 126
Cannan, Edwin, 58n
Cappa, Alberto, 11
Cassirer, Ernst, 22n
Causal laws, 19
Causal relations, 108